I0821933

World History

The French Revolution

The Power of the People

By Karen Diane Haywood

Portions of this book originally appeared in *The French Revolution* by Don Nardo.

Published in 2017 by
Lucent Press, an Imprint of Greenhaven Publishing, LLC
353 3rd Avenue
Suite 255
New York, NY 10010

Designer: Deanna Paternostro
Editor: Siyavush Saidian

Library of Congress Cataloging-in-Publication Data

Names: Haywood, Karon Diane, author.
Title: The French Revolution : the power of the people / Kuren Diane Haywood.
Description: New York : Lucent Press, [2017] | Series: World history | Includes bibliographical references and index.
Identifiers: LCCN 2016050351 (print) | LCCN 2016050597 (ebook) | ISBN 9781534560512 (library bound : alk. paper) | ISBN 9781534560529 (E-book)
Subjects: LCSH: France–History–Revolution, 1789-1799–Juvenile literature.
Classification: LCC DC148 . H284 2017 (print) | LCC DC148 (ebook) | DDC 944.04–dc23
LC record available at https://lccn.loc.gov/2016050351

Printed in the United States of America

CPSIA compliance information: Batch #CW17KL: For further information contact Greenhaven Publishing LLC, New York, New York at 1-844-317-7404.

Please visit our website, www.greenhavenpublishing.com. For a free color catalog of all our high-quality books, call toll free 1-844-317-7404 or fax 1-844-317-7405.

CONTENTS

Foreword

History books are often filled with names and dates—words and numbers for students to memorize for a test and forget once they move on to another class. However, what history books should be filled with are great stories, because the history of our world is filled with great stories. Love, death, violence, heroism, and betrayal are not just themes found in novels and movie scripts. They are often the driving forces behind major historical events.

When told in a compelling way, fact is often far more interesting—and sometimes far more unbelievable—than fiction. World history is filled with more drama than the best television shows, and all of it really happened. As readers discover the incredible truth behind the triumphs and tragedies that have impacted the world since ancient times, they also come to understand that everything is connected. Historical events do not exist in a vacuum. The stories that shaped world history continue to shape the present and will undoubtedly shape the future.

The titles in this series aim to provide readers with a comprehensive understanding of pivotal events in world history. They are written with a focus on providing readers with multiple perspectives to help them develop an appreciation for the complexity of the study of history. There is no set lens through which history must be viewed, and these titles encourage readers to analyze different viewpoints to understand why a historical figure acted the way they did or why a contemporary scholar wrote what they did about a historical event. In this way, readers are able to sharpen their critical-thinking skills and apply those skills in their history classes. Readers are aided in this pursuit by formally documented quotations and annotated bibliographies, which encourage further research and debate.

Many of these quotations come from carefully selected primary sources, including diaries, public records, and contemporary research and writings. These valuable primary sources helps readers hear the voices of those who directly experienced historical events, as well as the voices of biographers and historians who provide a unique perspective on familiar topics. Their voices all help history come alive in a vibrant way.

As students read the titles in this series, they are provided with clear context in the form of maps, timelines, and informative text. These elements give them the basic facts they need to fully appreciate the high drama that is history.

The study of history is difficult at times—not because of all the information that needs to be memorized, but because of the challenging questions it asks us. How could something as horrible as the Holocaust happen? Why would religious leaders use torture during the Inquisition? Why does ISIS have so many followers? The information presented in each title gives readers the tools they need to confront these questions and participate in the debates they inspire.

As we pore over the stories of events and eras that changed the world, we come to understand a simple truth: No one can escape being a part of history. We are not bystanders; we are active participants in the stories that are being created now and will be written about in history books decades and even centuries from now. The titles in this series help readers gain a deeper appreciation for history and a stronger understanding of the connection between the stories of the past and the stories they are part of right now.

SETTING THE SCENE: A TIMELINE

1756–1763

France and its allies fight Britain and its allies in the Seven Years' War; France loses.

1774

Louis XVI and Marie-Antoinette become king and queen of France.

1781

With French military assistance, the Americans defeat the British at Yorktown, essentially winning the American Revolution; France's involvement in this and the earlier Seven Years' War further depletes the royal treasury.

1789

The Third Estate's delegates declare themselves to be the National Assembly; a Paris mob storms and captures the Bastille, a 14th-century fortress-prison; the National Assembly adopts the Declaration of the Rights of Man and of the Citizen.

1790

The National Assembly passes the Civil Constitution of the Clergy, which reorganizes the Catholic Church under state control.

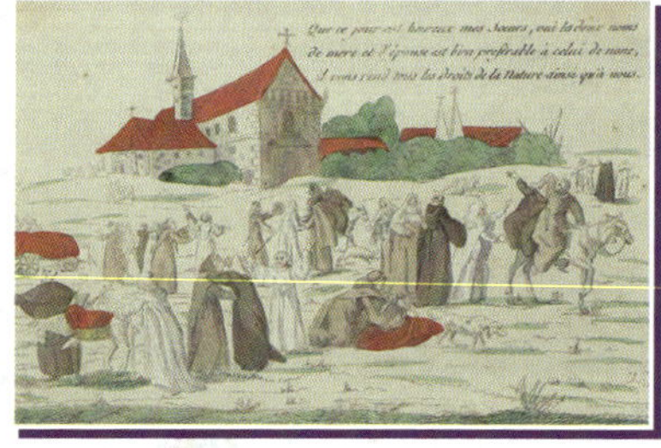

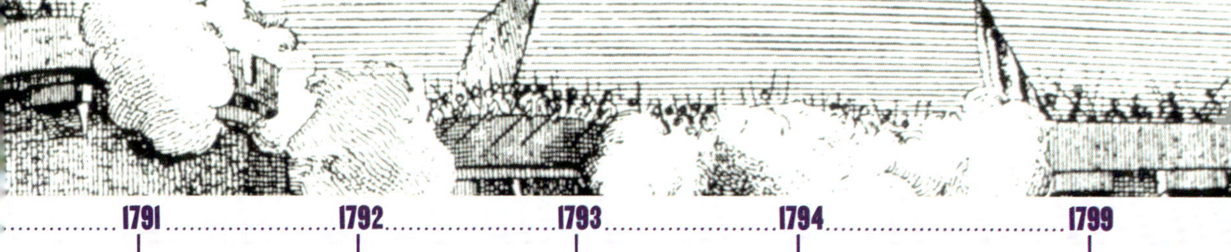

1791 1792 1793 1794 1799

1792

France declares war on Austria; the French monarchy is overthrown, and the First French Republic is declared; the Legislative Assembly orders the election of the National Convention; Robespierre is elected head of the National Convention.

1799

Napoléon names a new government and declares the French Revolution is over.

1794

Robespierre, chief architect of the Reign of Terror, is executed at the guillotine.

1791

Louis XVI and Marie-Antoinette try but fail to escape from France; the largest slave revolt in history begins on the French colony of Saint-Domingue (now Haiti).

1793

Louis XVI is condemned to death and beheaded three days later; Marie-Antoinette is charged with treason and executed.

INTRODUCTION

"MAN MAY BE FREE, IF HE RESOLVES TO BE SO"

As time passes, a number of social, political, and natural events can occur that affect the affairs of people, nations, or even the world for years to come. New nations declare their independence; popular or unpopular leaders come to and fall from power; battles are won and lost; social protests force new, more progressive laws to be enacted; famines, pandemics, oil spills, tornadoes, and other disasters destroy cities and devastate populations.

Rarely does a single event in one country radically change the course of history across most of the world for generations. The 20th century witnessed two such game-changers: the 1929 stock market crash, which initiated a devastating global economic depression, and the rise of Adolf Hitler, including Nazi Germany's invasion of Poland in 1939, which sparked World War II, the largest and deadliest war in history.

More than 100 years before either of these, the French Revolution made waves throughout Europe and the world. In one of the first uprisings of its kind, politicians and citizens alike united to force their way to liberty. They were inspired, in part, by Voltaire, an 18th-century philosopher. In his 1730 dramatic work *Brutus*, he wrote, "Man may be free, if he resolves to be so." It took years of fighting, both physically and intellectually, for France to realize this dream of freedom. However, in the 1790s, the French shook the world with their steadfast determination to achieve it.

Liberty, Equality, Fraternity

The French Revolution, which began in 1789, was every bit as momentous

Voltaire (1694–1778) was a writer, historian, and philosopher famous for his wit and his support for freedom of religion, freedom of expression, and separation of church and state.

as the above-mentioned events, and its consequences and influences were even more profound. "This great drama transformed the whole meaning of political change," historian William Doyle pointed out, "and the contemporary world would be inconceivable if it had not happened."[1]

Doyle emphasizes "political change" when describing the French Revolution for a good reason. Most earlier revolutions in world history did not drastically alter the political status quo. Thousands of people may have died and entire cities may have been looted or burned, but in most cases, the leaders who took charge ruled in the same manner and utilized the same political systems as those they had overthrown. With few exceptions, these systems were based on absolute monarchy. That is, a king, queen, emperor, or other monarch was in complete control of the nation. This control was centered on the divine right of kings, which claimed that reigning monarchs derived their authority to rule by the grace of God, not from the people, and were therefore infallible.

What made the French Revolution so different? It completely scrapped and swept aside France's centuries-old monarchy. Even the American Revolution, another major historical turning point that occurred a little more than a decade earlier, had not gone that far. True, the American rebels had shaken off British rule and set up their own nation, the United States, with a progressive political system in which the people elect their leaders. However, the Americans did not topple and eradicate Britain's monarchy and execute thousands of its citizens.

In contrast, that is exactly what happened in France. Between 1789 and 1794, the French people dethroned and arrested their king, Louis XVI, dismantled his monarchy, and executed him, his wife, and thousands of other nobles, clergy, and regular citizens. The revolutionaries replaced these leaders with a new system based on the then-radical concepts of popular rule, personal liberty, and equal justice for all.

After that, France was never the same. Since that time, its people and government have periodically undergone turmoil and wrestled with how best to serve the interests of the country and its population. Throughout it all, the ideals of the Revolution—liberty, equality, and fraternity (brotherhood)—have always remained sacred and fundamental. The French celebrate their independence day (July 14, when a French mob captured the monarchy's prison-fortress, the Bastille) with just as much pride as the Americans celebrate July 4.

This image shows a French citizen trying to capture liberty, equality, and fraternity while being watched closely by death. It was meant to symbolize the Revolution.

Revolution as Inspiration

Even more momentous, however, was the impact the French Revolution had on its European neighbors and, eventually, the rest of the globe. France's affairs and the aspirations of its leaders had long been intimately intertwined with those of other nations. It is no surprise that the destruction of its monarchy and the chaos caused by the Revolution sent shock waves throughout Europe and beyond. As the noted modern scholar Jacques Solé wrote, "Attitudes toward history and social order could no longer be the same after 1799 [the year the Revolution officially ended] as they had been before 1789. An ideological tidal wave, the French Revolution was, in this sense, the cradle of the modern world. Its long-range influence was to prove more important in this respect than in its immediate effects."[2]

Indeed, partly inspired by France's great rebellion, many other political revolutions and reform movements swept across Europe and the Americas in the 19th century. These forever changed the attitudes of those involved about how they should be ruled and helped to set the stage for the remarkable spread of democracy in the 20th century. "The shadow of the Revolution, therefore, fell across

This map shows France in 1795, four years before the end of the Revolution.

the whole of the nineteenth century and beyond," Doyle wrote. "Until 1917 [when the Russian Revolution began] few would have disputed that [the French Revolution] was the greatest revolution in the history of the world; and even after that its claims to primacy remain strong. It was the first modern revolution, the [model] one. After it, nothing in the European world remained the same, and we are all heirs to its influence."[3]

CHAPTER ONE

REVOLUTIONARY ORIGINS

Although the French Revolution and the American Revolution shared several common themes, they differed in many ways. Both had roots in the philosophical ideals of the Enlightenment, a movement that championed reason and reform to answer "how to redefine and rationalize the social order, how to change man in mind and heart."[4] Other similarities include the frustrations with unfair taxation and wealth distribution, hierarchical society, and the hereditary rule of an absolute monarchy.

With an ancient society came countless problems that had been bothering the French people for years, so there was not one simple cause for this event in human history. The French Revolution had many complex roots, but what is clear is that the people of France wanted to rule at home. They wanted to take away power from the monarchy and nobility and reform the system.

Just as there was no single cause for the Revolution, the Revolution was not a single event. As William Doyle wrote, it was "a series of developments, bewildering to most contemporaries, which stretched over a number of years."[5] Indeed, after its outbreak in 1789 and until its end 10 years later, the Revolution underwent several distinct phases, each with its own set of leaders, goals, and outcomes.

That its diverse causes came together and ignited enormous upheaval in France is not surprising. First, with almost 26 million people, the nation was by far the most populous in Europe. Thus, the French government had more people to keep track of, protect, appease, and control than its neighbors. If France's ability to appease and control its population

UNIFORMITY IN TAXATION

In a speech delivered in February 1787, France's chief finance minister, Charles-Alexandre de Calonne, advocated the principal of "uniformity" in taxation, that is, the idea that all French, regardless of social rank, should share the tax burden:

> *His Majesty has first of all considered the various forms of administration which occur in those provinces without [local] Estates. In order that the distribution of taxation may cease to be unequal and arbitrary, He has decided to confide the task to the landowners and he has derived from the first principles of the monarchy the general plan of a graduated series of deliberative assemblies whereby the expression of the taxpayers' wishes and their observations on everything which concerns them will be transmitted from parish to district assemblies, thence to provincial assemblies and through them to the throne.*
>
> *Next His Majesty brought all his personal attention to bear on establishing the same principle of uniformity … in the distribution of the land tax … by restoring the original intention behind the tax, and by raising it to its true value without increasing anyone's contribution (indeed granting some relief to the people).*[1]

Charles-Alexandre de Calonne, shown here, was France's chief finance minister from 1783 to 1787.

1. Quoted in "Calonne, 'Programs of Reform,' Address to the Assembly of Notables (1787)," Liberty, Equality, Fraternity: Exploring the French Revolution. chnm.gmu.edu/revolution/d/258/.

ever weakened, it would have more to lose.

France was also powerful and ambitious. It had an elaborate monarchy, many entrenched aristocratic institutions, a state-sponsored church, a large army and navy, and numerous foreign colonies and commitments, all of which were costly to maintain. Any inability to pay for them was bound to lead to instability—or worse.

Moreover, France was a major center of learning, intellectual debate, and new—sometimes radical—ideas. "Because there was more wealth [and] more [intellectual] enlightenment in France," historian Arthur J. May wrote, "Frenchmen were more dynamically discontented with the status quo, more ready for drastic changes."[6]

The Price of Monarchy, Imperialism, and War

Although revolution was not inevitable in 18th-century France, it was distinctly possible. All that was needed was a major setback to start a chain of events that could threaten the stability of its existing social and political order. One huge setback was a conflict fought from 1756 to 1763. In the Seven Years' War, France formed an alliance

The Battle of Quiberon Bay in 1759 was a decisive French defeat during the Seven Years' War.

with Russia, Austria, and Sweden and clashed with the combined forces of Britain and Prussia (Germany). The outcome was disastrous for France. Prussia routed France's land armies, and the British navy defeated French fleets on the high seas. Britain also pushed France out of India and North America (where the conflict was called the French and Indian War), except for some Caribbean islands where French colonies survived but suffered serious economic reversals. As a result, Britain emerged as the world's dominant colonial power.

These losses left France not only beaten and humiliated, but also financially strapped. The French government had borrowed heavily to finance the war, and now it was unclear how it was going to pay its gigantic debts. Just making the regular payments on them took more than half of the nation's tax revenues in the years immediately following the war. Making matters worse, French tax revenues were mostly below normal levels in the mid-1780s.

Incredibly, even in the face of these economic woes, in the 1770s, the French government again borrowed money to wage war. The new king, Louis XVI, who had succeeded his grandfather Louis XV to the throne in 1774, agreed to aid the Americans in their bid for independence from the British. Hoping to humble its archenemy, Britain, as well as regain some influence in North America, France sent ships and soldiers. These were instrumental in the American victory and the survival of the United States; however, though it gained prestige in the affair, France made no territorial gains and only fell further into debt.

Louis XVI succeeded his grandfather as king in 1774 at the age of 19.

The economic situation was dire when the bright and practical Charles-Alexandre de Calonne became France's chief finance minister in 1783. Calonne concluded that business as usual could not continue, because the existing system was broken. There was no national budget and little central financial planning. Large sums of money ended up in the hands of diverse high-ranking officials who answered mostly to themselves. Moreover, the French people were already badly overtaxed, so asking for more was not an option. Calonne told the king, "it is impossible to tax further, ruinous to be always borrowing ... With matters as they are ... the only course left to take, the only means of managing finally to put the finances truly in order, must consist in [reorganizing] the entire state."[7]

Calonne proposed a radical reform of most state institutions, government ministries, and the national tax system, making all of them more efficient. The result, he argued, would be far less waste and far more government income. In February 1787, the king convened a meeting of the Assembly of Notables with the most powerful national officials and aristocrats to consider Calonne's proposals. However, these men, the leaders of the sociopolitical order known as the ancien régime, were selfish and lacked vision. Fearing they would lose some or all of their power and wealth if the system changed, they sought to destroy the plan. King Louis lacked the will and fortitude to counter them.

This put France in a difficult, potentially dangerous situation. As one scholar pointed out, the country still possessed considerable national resources, which, properly used, could have put it on the road to recovery. However, many of these resources "were locked up by the system of government, the organization of society, and the culture" of the ancien régime. "It took the Revolution to release them."[8]

The Power of the French People

Another potential resource that remained locked up by the system was the power of the French people. They were mostly poor or lower–middle class and had long suffered blatant exploitation and unequal treatment under the old system of privilege. Indeed, the social structure of the ancien régime was highly class-oriented, inflexible, and often unjust. Over time, more and more average French men and women had become unhappy with the existing order. May explained that in other parts of Europe and in France, order

> *was anchored firmly on the assumption of human inequality. By reason of birth or calling, it was believed, [people] belonged to precise social castes in keeping with the will and the wish of the Almighty. Broadly speaking, there were two social categories: the privileged and the rest of humanity. The privileged element, in turn, was divided into the churchmen, or First Estate, and the aristocracy, the Second Estate ... More than twenty-four million Frenchmen, bourgeoisie [middle class], artisans, town laborers, and country folk, were grouped in the unprivileged "Third" Estate.*[9]

The Third Estate comprised close to 98 percent of the country's total population. The numbers of people in the other estates were much smaller, with about 100,000 clergy in the First Estate and about 400,000 nobles in the Second Estate.

The smallest of the three estates, the clergy, possessed a disproportionate amount of power, privilege, and influence. At least, this was true of the bishops and other high-ranking churchmen, who numbered fewer than a thousand. These men were recruited directly from the aristocracy. Used to wealth and privilege, they continued to collect fat incomes, lived in mansions or palaces, and were exempt from paying taxes. This mere handful of men also owned one-tenth of the land in France, some 20,000 square miles (51,800 sq. km). The average bishop spent most of his time enjoying the good life and knew little about his diocese and the needs and problems of its members.

Meanwhile, the lowly monks, nuns, and parish priests, who made little money, did most of the actual church work. In return, they were far more liked and respected than the high-ranking clergy members. Not surprisingly, most of the lower clergymen sided with the common people

This image depicts what it would be like if all three estates shared the burden of taxation.

during the Revolution.

The Second Estate, made up of the royal family and the nobles, was in many ways even more privileged than the high clergy. The king had a number of absolute powers that he believed were granted by God. At his own personal whim, the king could declare and wage war, dispense justice (including throwing anyone he pleased into prison without trial), conduct foreign policy, make new laws, and tax his subjects. He also owned large amounts of land to use for his own needs and pleasures. Hunting was a passion of the king, and he would often hunt on horseback or on foot around the perimeter of the palace. Later, hunting became a way for King Louis XVI to escape from the overwhelming crises occurring in his kingdom.

Louis XVI and Marie-Antoinette, shown here, greatly enjoyed hunting.

The degree to which these absolute powers and extensive privileges could be misused was exemplified by Louis XV, who ruled France from 1715 to 1774. Well-meaning, but incompetent and arrogant, he reasserted his ancestral authority in a 1766 speech: "It is to me alone that legislative power belongs ... The whole public order emanates from me, and the rights and interests of the nation ... are necessarily joined with mine and rest only in my hands."[10] He became widely disliked by most of his subjects.

The public image of the monarchy deteriorated even further under Louis's successor, Louis XVI. At first, the younger Louis and his queen, Marie-Antoinette, were popular, but the new king turned out to be slow-witted and indecisive, while Marie-Antoinette was thought to spend money frivolously and was nicknamed Madame Deficit. These royals eventually came to be seen as weak, wasteful, and symbols of a corrupt monarchy.

Self-indulgence and waste also became the hallmarks of the French aristocracy. The leading nobles, members of ancient upper-class families, lived on immense estates that generated huge yearly incomes. They alone were allowed to serve in the Church's highest offices and to command military units. They were also exempt from paying the taille, a direct tax that heavily burdened the peasants, and they possessed numerous ancient privileges, including control of local courts, rentals of land and houses, hunting rights, corn mills, wine presses, and bread ovens. The extensive privileges that wealthy lords enjoyed were among the many feudal obligations the peasants traditionally owed these nobles. Most lords kept detailed records of peasant families and the obligations they owed. These records gave the nobles legal leverage and the upper hand when disputes occurred.

Only one major wedge divided the king from the hereditary nobles. To keep these traditional aristocrats from gaining too much state power, previous French kings had elevated the rank of a few middle-class families, which created a small but powerful new aristocracy. Almost all of the king's chief ministers came from this group, whose members the older landed nobles (those who owned large amounts of land) resented.

The Social Order

The many feudal and other privileges enjoyed by France's king and nobles were frequently exacted at the expense of commoners, the members of the Third Estate, which was divided into two rather distinct groups. The middle class (bourgeoisie), made up a small percentage of the Third Estate and included merchants, moneylenders, shipowners, shopkeepers, artisans, lawyers, doctors, and writers. Some made only moderate livings, while others were well-off. They all shared the burdens of high taxes and low social status, both of which they hated with a passion. Members of the middle class wanted to live in a society in which money and merit, not birth, determined social rank and privilege. (This wish would be partly fulfilled, as men from the bourgeoisie would end up largely running the Revolution.)

The rest of the Third Estate included the peasants, who made up the bulk of the population. The peasants did most of the menial labor, paid most of the taxes, and lived basic, poor, and uncertain lives. A majority

Shown here is a typical peasant family preparing food for dinner.

of them, May wrote, "operated only small farms, sufficient merely to supply the necessities of their personal families, if indeed that. [Other peasants] hired themselves out as day laborers. Underemployment was a chronic evil in rural France. When crop yields were short, many poor peasants were reduced to beggary or actually starved."[11]

DIVIDING THE GOVERNMENT

Frenchman Charles-Louis de Secondat, baron de La Brède et de Montesquieu, was among the more influential thinkers of the Enlightenment. In his 1748 treatise *The Spirit of the Laws* he argued that a just government should be divided into three independent parts—the legislative, executive, and judicial:

> *When legislative power is united with executive power in a single person or in a single body of the magistracy, there is no liberty, because one can fear that the same monarch or senate that makes tyrannical laws will execute them tyrannically. Nor is there liberty if the power of judging is not separate from legislative power and from executive power. If it were joined to legislative power, the power over the life and liberty of the citizens would be arbitrary, for the judge would be the legislator. If it were joined to executive power, the judge could have the force of an oppressor. All would be lost if the same man or the same body of principal men ... exercised these three powers, that of making laws, that of executing public resolutions, and that of judging the crimes or the disputes of individuals.*[1]

1. Quoted in Diane Ravitch and Abigail Thernstrom, eds., *The Democracy Reader: Classic and Modern Speeches, Essays, Poems, Declarations, and Documents on Freedom and Human Rights Worldwide*. New York, NY: HarperCollins, 1992, p. 41.

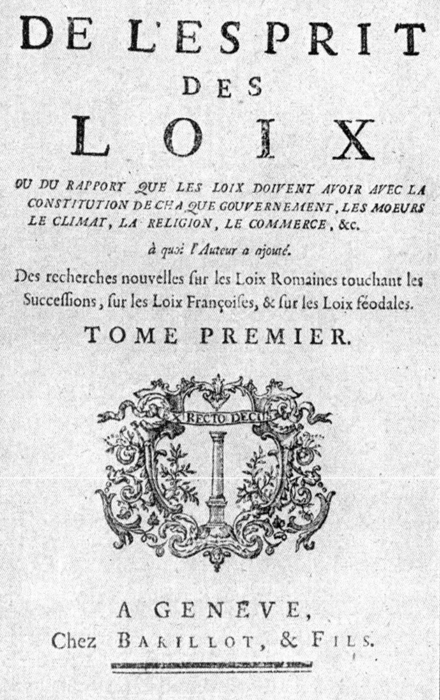

DE L'ESPRIT DES LOIX

OU DU RAPPORT QUE LES LOIX DOIVENT AVOIR AVEC LA CONSTITUTION DE CHAQUE GOUVERNEMENT, LES MOEURS LE CLIMAT, LA RELIGION, LE COMMERCE, &c.

à quoi l'Auteur a ajouté.

Des recherches nouvelles sur les Loix Romaines touchant les Successions, sur les Loix Françoises, & sur les Loix féodales.

TOME PREMIER.

A GENEVE,

Chez BARILLOT, & FILS.

In The Spirit of the Laws, *published anonymously in Amsterdam, Montesquieu called for a constitutional system of government, the separation of powers, abolishing slavery, universal civil liberties, and the rule of equitable laws.*

These difficulties and inequalities within France's traditional social order had been a source of discontent for a long time, but most people had simply accepted them as inevitable and unchangeable. As the country's financial problems worsened at all levels throughout the mid-1700s, however, tensions within all social classes grew more pronounced. "The French social pyramid was riddled with contradictions both within and between its constituent parts," scholar George Rudé explained. It had

> *an aristocracy that, though privileged and mostly wealthy, was deeply resentful of its long exclusion from [high state] office; a bourgeoisie that, though enjoying increasing prosperity, was denied the social status ... commensurate with [equal to] its wealth; and peasants who (in part at least) were becoming more literate and independent, yet were still regarded as a general beast of burden, despised and over-taxed. Moreover, these conflicts and the tensions they engendered were becoming sharper as the century went on.*[12]

The Argument for Basic Human Rights

Also contributing to the growth of discontent in 18th-century France was the spread of new social and philosophical ideas that challenged the legitimacy of the old order. These ideas sprang from what came to be known as the Enlightenment. It was a movement of thinkers and writers, most of them English and French, who strongly influenced people and institutions throughout Europe and the Americas. These thinkers (referred to as "philosophes" in France) called for the universal adoption of certain rights they argued are basic. Among them are religious freedom, including the separation of church and state; fair, just, representative government; and freedom of speech and expression. They also stressed the importance of reason, science, and regular social and political reform in the creation of a more enlightened society and world.

Chief among the French Enlightenment thinkers were Francois-Marie Arouet, better known as Voltaire, Denis Diderot, Charles-Louis de Secondat, baron de La Brède et de Montesquieu, and Jean-Jacques Rousseau. These men argued that the Church was corrupt and should be reformed; all human beings are by nature equal, are good (though subject to corruption), and have the right to control their own destiny; and the principal role of a nation's government is to meet the needs of its citizens.

Such ideas, then widely viewed as radical, found fertile soil for growth in France. There, scholar John H. Stewart wrote, the middle class was extremely "desirous of change."[13] Moreover, many of its members were literate

Denis Diderot, shown here, was a French philosopher and writer who embraced the spirit of the Enlightenment.

and eagerly read and discussed the writings of the philosophes. These writings reached the people through a number of outlets, Stewart pointed out. "Coffee shops provided meeting places where people might discuss current trends, where news could be disseminated [spread], [and] where even the illiterate could learn what was taking place. Masonic lodges [private clubs] likewise afforded an excellent [atmosphere] for the exchange of ideas and opinions."[14] Other important outlets for exchanging news and ideas included France's many salons (gatherings of literary and artistic people) and the distribution of short, but often controversial, pamphlets. The latter, Stewart wrote, "could be written and printed rapidly, circulated inexpensively, and passed easily from reader to reader."[15]

Overall, in the late 1780s, the French people were unhappy with the way things were, and some of them had strong ideas about alternative systems. The question was not whether change would come, but rather how and when it would happen. As it turned out, it happened sooner than anyone expected. The king needed money badly, and he decided to ask his people for help. He did not realize that this seemingly harmless act would lead to his untimely death and the transformation of the society he had known.

CHAPTER TWO

POLITICAL AWAKENING OF 1789

In 1788, France was suffering from food shortages, uprisings, a long spring drought followed by deadly hailstorms, and a failing economy. Panic seized the stock market as government funds nosedived and there was a run on the principal bank. The debt crisis dovetailed with ever-increasing public criticism of privilege and the extravagant lifestyles of the monarchy and nobility. One finance minister after another advised the king that there was only one viable, realistic way to restore the health of the royal treasury: He must tax the vast lands owned by the nobility and the church. Both groups had long been exempt from land taxes and had no intention of paying them now, regardless of the state of the treasury and the social unrest in the nation. They politely, but forcefully, pointed out that the only legal way the king could impose such taxes was to convene a meeting of the Estates-General.

The Estates-General was an impermanent gathering of delegates elected by the three estates; it last met in 1614, 160 years before Louis XVI became king. Such a council generally met only in dire situations when the king and his ministers had no other choice.

The First and Second Estates assumed the king had more to lose than to gain by calling such a gathering, as it would allow the members of the Third Estate to present their list of grievances to the government. Also, the king had enough problems to deal with without creating more.

However, Louis was in such desperate need of money that he proceeded to call the bluff of the nobles and bishops. Late in 1788, at his current finance minister's insistence, he agreed to call the

This painting shows an onlooker's view of the meeting of the Estates-General in 1789.

Estates-General to Paris the following May. His official summons of January 1789 for the council said in part:

> *Beloved and loyal supporters, we require the assistance of our faithful subjects to overcome the difficulties in which we find ourselves concerning the current state of our finances, and to establish, as we so wish, a constant and invariable order in all branches of government that concern the happiness of our subjects and the prosperity of the realm. These great motives have induced us to summon the Assembly of the Estates of all Provinces [the Estates-General] obedient to us ... to inform us of the wishes and grievances of our people.*[16]

With these words, Louis unwittingly set in motion a chain reaction he would be powerless to stop.

The Power of the Press

Just as the nobles and churchmen had underestimated Louis, he now made the same mistake in regard to the Third Estate. Evidently, he thought that its representatives would obediently come to Paris and present a few minimal grievances, he would make a show of promising to address them, and they would approve his plan to levy new taxes on the wealthy and then go home.

What the king did not foresee was that the Third Estate may not want to dutifully bow to him and leave. It did not occur to him that its members might assert themselves against the established order. Perhaps

THE NOBILITY UNDER ATTACK

One of the most provocative pamphlets circulating in France in the months prior to the Revolution was *What is the Third Estate?* by the outspoken Abbé Sieyès. In this section, he attacks the aristocratic class and its traditional privileges:

> *It is not possible in the number of all the elementary parts of a nation to find a place for the caste of nobles ... The worst possible arrangement of all would be where not alone isolated individuals, but a whole class of citizens should take pride in remaining motionless in the midst of the general movement, and should consume the best part of the product without bearing any part in its production. Such a class is surely estranged to the nation by its indolence ...*
>
> *[Is it] not evident that the noble order has privileges and expenditures which it dares to call its rights, but which are apart from the rights of the great body of citizens? It departs there from the common order, from the common law. So its civil rights make of it an isolated people in the midst of the great nation.*[1]

1. Quoted in "Sieyès: 'What Is the Third Estate?' (1789)," Liberty, Equality, Fraternity: Exploring the French Revolution. chnm.gmu.edu/revolution/d/280/.

QU'EST-CE QUE

LE

TIERS-ÉTAT?

TROISIÈME ÉDITION.

« Tant que le *Philosophe* n'excède point les limites de la vérité, ne l'accusez pas d'aller trop loin. Sa fonction est de marquer le but, il faut donc qu'il y soit arrivé. Si restant en chemin, il osoit y élever son enseigne, elle pourroit être trompeuse. Au contraire, le devoir de l'*Administrateur* est de *combiner* et de *graduer* sa marche, suivant la nature des difficultés..... Si le Philosophe n'est au but, il ne sait où il est. Si l'Administrateur ne voit le but, il ne sait où il va. »

1789.

Faksimile des Titels von Sieyes' Schrift „Qu'est-ce que le Tiers-État?

Shown here is the title page of the controversial What is the Third Estate? *pamphlet that was distributed months before the Revolution.*

partly because the monarchy had, by habit, insulated itself from life among the commoners, the king did not realize that powerful forces had been unleashed in the form of the people's raised hopes. Many French saw the upcoming meeting as a sign that the government was ready to hear and remedy their grievances. Some even dared to hope that they would take part in instituting a new, fairer sociopolitical system. To them, the royal summons to the Estates-General "was a recognition of the fact that reform was imperative," historian R.K. Gooch wrote. "It was also a recognition of the fact that the king could not, without the collaboration of the nation, effect real reform ... The king's acceptance, however reluctant, of the direction and force of public opinion aroused high hopes in the country."[17]

These expectations that the upcoming meeting might bring positive reforms were expressed in numerous gatherings of small groups of citizens in the cities and towns. People's hopes and optimism about the meeting also manifested themselves in the circulation of hundreds, perhaps even thousands, of pamphlets. Arthur Young, an English landowner who was staying in France at this time observed:

> *The business going forward at present in the pamphlet shops is incredible ... Every hour produces something new. Thirteen came out to-day, sixteen yesterday, and ninety-two last week ... The spirit of reading political tracts, they say, spreads into the provinces, so that all the presses of France are equally employed ... It is easy to conceive the spirit that must thus be raised among the people. But the coffee-houses ... present yet more singular and astonishing spectacles; they are not only [crowded] within, but other expectant [crowds] are at the doors and windows listening ... to certain orators ... The eagerness with which they are heard, and the thunder of applause they receive for every sentiment ... against the present government, cannot easily be imagined.*[18]

Radical and Provocative Ideas

The representatives of the three estates gathered in Paris in early May 1789 at Versailles, a palace about 12 miles (19 km) outside the city. It was on this day that Louis made his first serious mistake. Forgetting, or perhaps not caring, that he was dealing from a position of weakness and badly needed the commoners' support, he treated them poorly. First, he warmly, with pomp and ceremony, greeted the delegates of the nobility and clergy in the Hall of Mirrors. Then, to emphasize they were inferior, he rudely kept the delegates of the Third Estate waiting for three hours. When he finally met with them in a less glamorous room, he maintained a cold, aloof posture as they filed by him one by one.

The Hall of Mirrors at Versailles is where Louis XVI greeted the clergy and nobles, but he met the Third Estate in a much less lavish part of the palace.

According to noted scholar of the Revolution, Christopher Hibbert, "The king, standing between his two brothers, could not bring himself to address a single word to any of them other than one old man of exceptionally benign appearance, to whom he said, 'Good morning, good man.' The others, having made their bows, turned away, feeling much disheartened by the King's inability to display the least indication of friendliness."[19]

It is possible that King Louis's incivility was due in part to the fact that he was not looking forward to hearing the commoners' complaints. He was aware, after all, that they had come bearing *cahiers de doléances*—lists of grievances—that they expected him to consider in exchange for supporting his tax initiative. These grievances, compiled in various towns across the realm, included numerous and diverse requests and demands. Typical were appeals for regular meetings of the Estates-General, lower taxes, and freedom of the press. Concerning the last of these, a group of commoners from Paris declared that "liberty of the press must be granted, on condition that authors sign their manuscripts, that the printer's name shall appear, and that both shall be responsible for the consequences of publication."[20]

Another grievance, from the town of Vire (located several miles west of Paris), asked for a more even-handed justice system. "Justice [should] be free of charge [and] civil and criminal edicts [should] be reformed [and] crime alone, and not the social standing of the criminal, [should] determine the sentence, and ... no citizen may, under the pretext of any [social or aristocratic] privilege ... be brought before any other than his natural judge."[21] Such requests, though somewhat daring for the time, were actually among the tamer ideas and statements circulating among the crowds of commoners.

Emmanuel Joseph Sieyès (commonly called Abbé Sieyès since he was a Catholic clergyman), a delegate of and spokesman for the Third Estate, had recently published a pamphlet titled *What is the Third Estate?* In it, he fiercely defended the commoners of France as the foundation of the French nation and the most productive part of society, building on the Enlightenment emphasis on useful citizens. Many of the delegates had read it, and they agreed with its major points, including these bold and provocative ones:

> *Who then shall dare to say that the Third Estate has not within itself all that is necessary for the formation of a complete nation? It is the strong and robust man who has one arm still shackled. If the privileged order should be abolished, the nation would be nothing less, but something more. Therefore, what is the Third Estate? Everything; but an everything shackled and oppressed. What would it be without the privileged order? Everything, but an everything free and flourishing. Nothing can succeed without it, everything would be infinitely better without the others.*
>
> *It is not sufficient to show that privileged persons, far from being useful to the nation, cannot but enfeeble and*

Emmanuel Joseph Sieyès, active in the Revolution from the beginning until the end, was one of the few radicals to not be condemned to the guillotine.

CAHIERS DE DOLÉANCES

The 60,000 *cahiers*, or lists of grievances, drawn up by local groups of citizens and presented to the government at the Estates-General, were highly progressive and controversial for their time, as explained by one of the leading scholars of the Revolution, William Doyle:

> *The* cahiers *produced a picture of the outlook and preoccupations of a whole nation unique in Europe before the twentieth century. And the very fact of being asked to articulate their grievances and aspirations (with the implicit promise of redress) concentrated the minds of everybody involved on the seriousness of what was at stake ... The drafting of the* cahiers *drew in people throughout the country. The [local] elections of [representatives to the Estates-General in] 1789 were the most democratic spectacle ever seen in the history of Europe, and nothing comparable occurred again until far into the next century.*[1]

1. William Doyle, *The Oxford History of the French Revolution*. Oxford, UK: Clarendon, 2002, p. 97.

> *injure it. It is necessary to prove further that the noble order does not enter at all into the social organization; that it may indeed be a burden upon the nation, but that it cannot of itself constitute a nation.*[22]

New Rules in the Age of Reason

Before the people's grievances could be formally presented, however, the delegates of the three estates had to agree on acceptable rules for debate and voting. Before this step could be taken, tradition dictated that the delegates' credentials had to be examined and verified. This formality was designed to make sure that every person at the meeting had been properly chosen by his peers for this important task. At their last meeting, in 1614, each estate had briefly met separately and checked the credentials of its own members. Now, in 1789, the nobles and churchmen proceeded to do the same.

However, the delegates of the Third Estate were uncomfortable with the procedure. First, how could they be sure that what went on in the other two meetings was fair? Also, they argued, if the Estates-General truly represented the entire realm, should not everyone's credentials be open to examination by all three estates? Following this reasoning, the commoners refused to present their credentials until the other two estates agreed to an open process.

There was also a lot of talk among the commoners about voting procedure for the convention. In the past, each estate had had a single, collective voice amounting to one vote. Not surprisingly, aiming to maintain their monopoly on power, the nobles and clergy had always voted together, two to one, against the Third Estate. The commoners strongly objected to this approach and now voiced this concern. They demanded that the rules be changed to give a vote to each and every delegate of the convention. Because the nobles had 291 delegates, the clergy 300, and the commoners 610, that would give the Third Estate a majority voice.

When it looked as if the nobles and clergy were not going to bend on the credentials and voting issues, the members of the Third Estate became increasingly irritated and bold. They made overtures to members of the first two estates, asking them to join the third. A group of commoners went to the churchmen's meeting and said, "the gentlemen of the Commons invite the gentlemen of the clergy, in the name of the God of Peace and for the national interest, to meet them in their hall to consult upon the means of bringing about the concord [peaceful agreement] which is so vital at this moment for the public welfare."[23]

At first, these invitations went unanswered. However, in June 1789, the earnest and by now quite impatient Sieyès proposed that the commoners strike out on their own. If the other two estates would not join the third, he said, they should forfeit their rights to speak for the nation. This bold move had the desired effect as liberal nobles and clergymen from the First and Second Estates joined them. At first, it was a small amount: three one day followed by six more shortly after.

THE NATIONAL ASSEMBLY IS BORN

After deciding to take matters into their own hands and form a national legislative body, the revolutionaries next took up the issue of what to call that body. Some of the delegates proposed they should call themselves The General Assembly. Another suggestion was Representatives of the French People and another, the mouthful: The Legimate Assembly of the Representatives of the Greater Part of the Nation, Acting in the Absence of the Smaller Part. Similar suggestions included The Assembly of the Representatives, known and verified of the French Nation and National Constituent Assembly. Finally, the delegates voted to adopt the far simpler National Assembly.

However, within a few days, 149 more joined the Third Estate.

The Revolution Begins

Emboldened, the delegates of the Third Estate now reasoned that their ranks no longer represented only the commoners. Rather, in their view, they stood for the wishes and rights of the vast majority of French of all classes. On June 17, in the name of the French people, they took the extraordinary step of issuing a short document in which they declared their body to be the National Assembly of France. "In a few deliberate and coldly logical phrases," scholar Leo Gershoy wrote, "they set aside the entire theory and practice of a government and society based upon privileged orders and asserted the democratic theory of [greater] numbers and of popular sovereignty."[24] Among these bold phrases were the following:

> *This Assembly is already composed of representatives sent directly by at least ninety-six one-hundredths [96 percent] of the nation ... Thus, the Assembly declares that the common work of national restoration can and must be initiated without delay by the deputies present, and that they must continue without interruption and without obstacle.*[25]

In the wake of this clearly revolutionary act, shock waves rippled across the capital and, in the days that followed, throughout the nation and beyond. Perhaps sensing the popular will, a majority of the priests, along with a handful of aristocrats from the Second Estate, joined the new National Assembly on June 19. Meanwhile, the king and his ministers, not to mention the leading nobles, were shocked and even fearful. Some urged the king to send in troops to disband the National Assembly and arrest its leaders.

However, King Louis thought that such a show of force could turn them into martyrs and thereby help their cause. So he took the less confrontational approach of depriving them of their meeting place. On June 20, when the National Assembly's members arrived at their hall, they found the doors locked and guarded by soldiers.

Undaunted, however, the delegates hurried to a nearby indoor tennis court. There, they swore never to disband until their self-appointed task of reforming the nation was finished. That declaration, which appropriately became known as the "Tennis Court Oath," read in part:

> *The National Assembly, considering that it has been called to establish the constitution of the realm, to bring about the regeneration of public order, and to maintain the true principles of the monarchy, nothing may prevent it from continuing its deliberations in any place it is forced to establish itself and, finally, the National Assembly ex-*

The Tennis Court Oath is shown here being read to the National Assembly.

ists wherever its members are gathered [and] decrees that all members of this assembly immediately take solemn oath never to separate, and to reassemble whenever circumstances require, until the constitution of the realm is drawn up and fixed upon solid foundations; and that said oath having been sworn, all members in general, and each one individually confirm this unwavering resolution with his signature.[26]

From the viewpoint of these brave men at that historic moment, the die had been cast. Unable to predict what might happen next, they were ready to suffer any consequences for what they saw as the good of their country. From the viewpoint of posterity, the French Revolution had begun.

Chapter Three

BLOODY REVOLUTION

When he heard the news, Louis XVI scorned the Third Estate's commitment to the people to represent all of France, dismissed the actions and declarations of the newly organized National Assembly, and belittled the name as simply a phrase. However, it was more than a phrase: It was a revolutionary act that laid the foundation for the country's upcoming experiment in representative democracy.

Well aware that they had defied the king by claiming sovereignty and the political right to govern by taking sovereignty from the king and transferring it themselves, the new National Assembly swore not to disband until they had reformed the government.

At this point, the revolutionaries had no overt intention of transforming France into a democracy. Also, they did not plan, nor did they even contemplate, abolishing the monarchy. Rather, their main goal was to draft a written constitution that would guarantee all French citizens, regardless of social class, basic civil rights. Then, they strongly hoped, the king would approve the document. France would thereafter be a constitutional monarchy, in which the king's authority rested on the will of the people and their legislative representatives. In short, the commoner deputies were optimistic that the government could and would be reformed in a peaceful manner.

It is unfortunate that this nonviolent scenario may well have happened had it not been for the king's arrogance and lack of vision. Although he was willing to make a few minor concessions to the deputies, he arrogantly reminded all involved

LOST OPPORTUNITY

When he met with the delegates of the Estates-General on June 23, 1789, King Louis promised a number of reforms that he was never able to implement because of the Revolution. Among others, these reforms included:

> *No new tax shall be created and no current tax will be extended beyond the term set by law and without consent of the nation's representatives ... Once the formal arrangements announced by clergy and nobility to renounce their financial privileges have been fixed ... the king intends to sanction them so that there will be no more privileges or distinctions in the payment of financial contributions ... All property, without exception, will be respected ... His majesty will examine (with scrupulous attention) all projects presented to him concerning the administration of justice and the means to perfect civil and criminal laws.*[1]

1. Quoted in Georges Lefebvre and Anne Terroine, eds., *Recueil de Documents Relatifs aux Séances des États- Généraux, Vol. 1*. trans. Laura Mason. Paris, France: National Center of Scientific Research, 1962, pp. 278–279.

that he was still the king and had the final word. There was only so far that he was willing to bend. As both sides refused to retreat from their stated positions, tension steadily rose. Inevitably, violence broke out, transforming what had been a peaceful rebellion into a bloody one.

Royal Concessions

King Louis's inability to grasp the true scope and gravity of the situation, as well as his inflexibility and lack of wisdom as a ruler, are well illustrated by his actions in the days following the Tennis Court Oath. He failed to recognize that the men who had sworn not to disband were not merely a small, isolated group of discontented commoners. Rather, they increasingly had the support of and spoke for thousands, even millions, of resentful French, such as the citizens who were marching in the streets due to rising bread and flour prices.

Apparently unable to see the big picture, King Louis assumed he could ease the crisis by giving in to a few of the delegates' demands while firmly reasserting what he viewed as his legitimate, God-given authority over them.

To this end, the king scheduled a meeting between himself and the delegates of the three estates on June 23, three days after the Tennis Court Oath. King Louis's entrance into the hall was accompanied by a lavish fanfare of trumpets and rolling drums. The gathered nobles and some of the clergy cheered him, but the commoners stood silent. Then he launched into a long prepared speech, which began with a reminder of his good intentions:

> *I believed that I had done everything in my power for the good of my people when I resolved to assemble you … when I anticipated the desires of the nation, so to speak, in declaring in advance what I wanted to do for its happiness … I owe it to the common good of my realm, [and] I owe it to myself to bring an end to these fatal divisions. In this conviction, Gentlemen, I have assembled you once more before me. As the common father of my subjects, as the defender of the laws of my realm, I come to [remind you of the] true spirit [of the laws] and to put an end to the harm that may have been inflicted upon it.*[27]

As the gathered delegates listened, King Louis offered to negotiate a series of reforms. The Estates-General would be allowed to meet on a regular basis and would have a number of financial powers. For instance, no new taxes would hereafter be imposed without the representatives' consent. Further, the Estates-General would prepare a sort of annual national budget of revenues and expenses, although it would be subject to the king's approval. The nobles and clergy would renounce their ancient financial privileges, and all French citizens would be taxed in the same manner. Louis went on to say that "the Estates-General will examine and make known to His Majesty the most suitable means of reconciling liberty of the press with the respect due to religion, morals, and the honor of citizens."[28]

These and the king's other concessions and remarks completely ignored the existence of the new National Assembly. King Louis was simply proposing that, except for the reforms he had just outlined, things should return to the way they had stood in May, before the Third Estate had asserted itself. Also, to emphasize

Louis XVI is shown here in formal attire.

that he was still in charge, he now reaffirmed his own authority. The three estates were to continue, per custom, to meet separately to discuss most matters. Moreover, the delegates had no right to draw up a constitution on their own, as it would be an invalid, illegal document. "None of your projects, none of your arrangements," he said, "can have the force of law without my special approbation [approval]. I am the natural guarantor of your respective rights."[29]

After finishing his speech, the king ordered everyone to leave and attend their separate meetings. Then he departed, followed by most members of the first two estates. However, the revolutionaries remained in the hall in defiance of the order. One of their leaders, Honoré-Gabriel Riqueti, comte de Mirabeau, told Louis's deputy, "Go tell your master that we are here by the will of the people and that we shall not stir from our seats unless forced to do so by bayonets."[30]

A Dangerous Situation

On hearing about the delegates' disobedience, King Louis showed restraint and did nothing. (An alternate account claims that he ordered soldiers to clear out the hall. If this was the case, they arrived after the delegates had left.) Clearly, he was unsure about how to deal with the continued defiance of his subjects, something he had never encountered before. His frustration and feelings of impotence further increased a few days later when several more clergymen and another 47 nobles joined the revolutionaries. In addition, rumors began to circulate in the capital that if he did not agree to allow all the estates to meet together, thousands of protestors might surround his palace. So, on June 27, he gave in and announced that he would allow such joint meetings.

At this point, the rebels had dramatically changed France's sociopolitical order in only a few weeks. They had done so without resorting to violence, and the king had offered only marginal interference. Had nothing else occurred to change this unfolding scenario, everyone's needs and demands may have been met over time. Large-scale bloodshed may have been avoided.

However, King Louis proceeded to make a more forceful stand, which, under the circumstances, was bound to lead to a dangerous situation. Perhaps he feared losing his great power and wealth. Certainly some members of the royal family and a few disgruntled noblemen felt this way. They strongly urged the king to use the army to enforce his will, and he did.

In late June, the king ordered four regiments of soldiers to advance on Paris and Versailles. Soon afterward, he called up several additional regiments, activating a force of some 30,000 soldiers in all. These regiments included many Swiss and German mercenaries—hired foreign soldiers.

News of the approaching troops swiftly spread through the capital, significantly raising levels of tension and fear—tension already heightened by the scarcity of bread. Rumors circulated of an aristocratic plot to hoard grain, and this is when the false rumor first arose that Marie-Antoinette said, "If they have no bread let them eat cake."

The leaders of the Revolution were genuinely worried that the soldiers might disband the National Assembly or maybe even ransack the city. In a speech to the National Assembly on July 8, Mirabeau railed: "A large number of troops already surround us! More are arriving each day. Artillery are being brought up ... These preparations for war are obvious to anyone and fill every heart with indignation."[31]

Meanwhile, hungry Parisians were paying attention to the political negotiations and stagnation happening at Versailles. They knew that, in the event the king outlawed the National Assembly, they had one hope beyond their delegates, someone who could lower the price of bread, which was at its highest level in 20 years—the king's current finance minister, the populist Jacques Necker. Along with the grain supply, they believed he would protect the National Assembly. Then, on July 11, the king fired Necker. As the news reached the capital the next afternoon, Parisians swarmed the streets.

Jacques Necker, finance minister, was considered the last, best hope for the Third Estate.

The revolutionary mood of optimism and hope for reform was giving way to the politics of hunger and fear. As worries about an imminent attack on the city increased, many felt they should mount some sort of defense. This meant that they must arm themselves, if possible, with muskets and cannons. In the next few days, the city streets—already filled with protesters, speechmakers, and many confused, frightened people—became even more chaotic as groups of citizens searched for guns and ammunition. Pierre-Victor Besenval was

A BASTILLE VETERAN REMEMBERS

In the crowd of Parisians who marched on the Bastille on July 14, 1789, was a man named Keversau, who later recalled the following events:

> *Veteran armies ... have never performed greater [examples] of valour than this leaderless multitude ... workmen of all trades who, mostly ill-equipped and unused to arms, boldly affronted the fire from the ramparts and seemed to mock the thunderbolts the enemy hurled at them ... The attackers having demolished the first drawbridge and brought their guns into position against the second, could not fail to capture the fort ... The people infuriated by the treachery of the Governor, who had fired on their representatives ... continued to advance, firing as they went up to the drawbridge leading to the interior of the fort. A Swiss officer addressing the attackers through a sort of loop-hole near the drawbridge asked permission to leave the fort with the honours of war. "No, no," they cried ... About two minutes later one of the [guards] opened the gate behind the drawbridge and asked what we wanted. "The surrender of the Bastille," was the answer, on which he let us in.*[1]

1. Quoted in Georges Pernoud and Sabine Flaissier, eds., *The French Revolution.* trans. Richard Graves. New York, NY: Capricorn, 1961, pp. 31–35

commander of Paris's permanent garrison of royal troops at the time. At first, he considered using his men to break up the protests and clear the streets. However, when he realized the magnitude of the crowds and unrest, he thought better of it and ordered the soldiers not to interfere unless fired on. These troops, he later recalled,

> *were the target of insulting cries, stone-throwing and pistol-shots. Several men were severely wounded, but not a single menacing gesture was made by the soldiers, so great was their respect for the order that not a drop of their fellow-citizens' blood was to be shed. The disorder increased hourly and with it my misgivings. What decision was I to take? If I engaged my troops in Paris, I should start a civil war. Blood, precious from whatever veins it flowed, would be shed without achieving any result likely to restore calm.*[32]

The July 14 Attacks

By July 14, some of those searching for weapons had become desperate. After taking a dozen cannons and about 30,000 firearms, but no gunpowder, from the Hôtel National des Invalides,

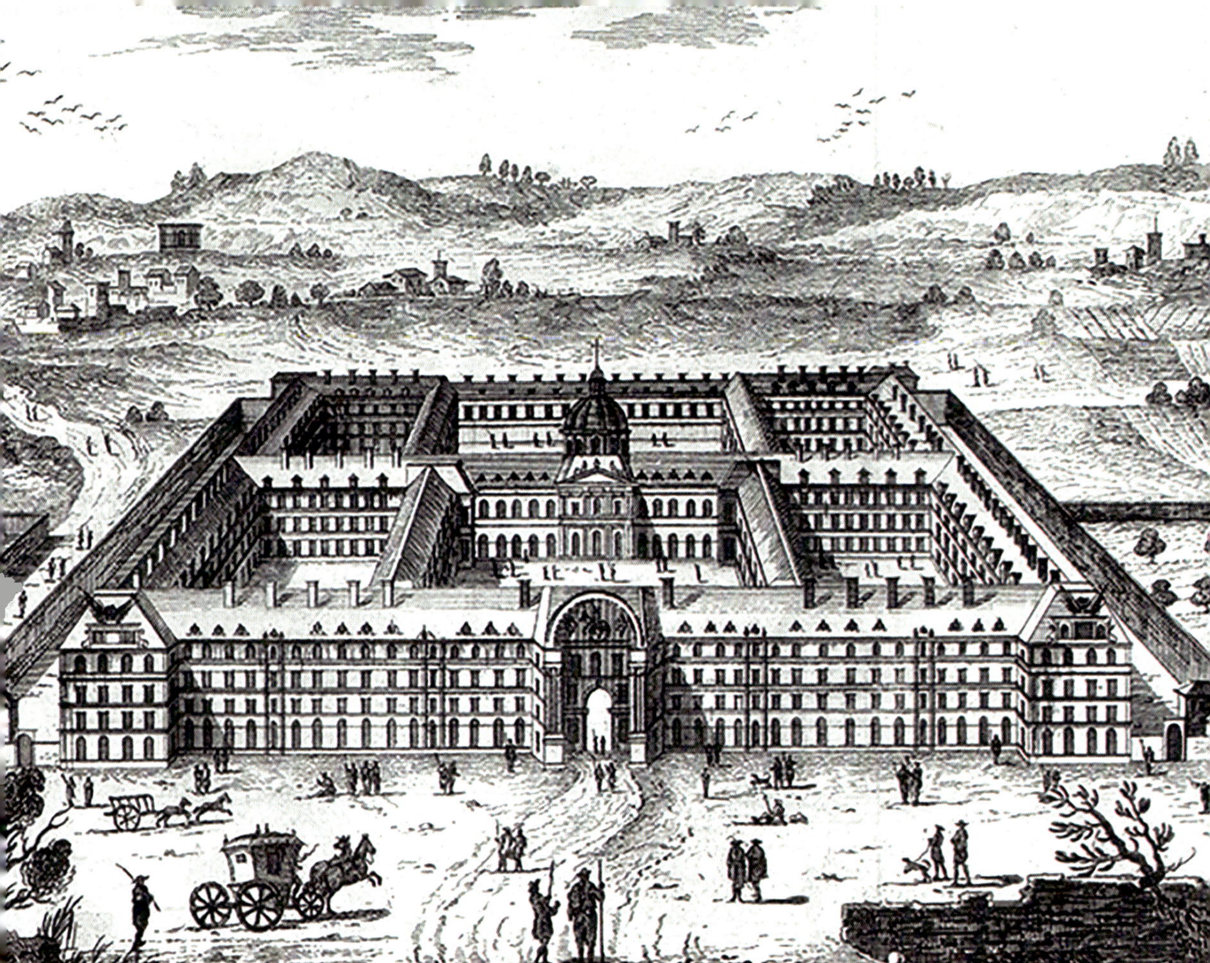

On July 14, 1789, Parisian rioters took cannons and muskets stored in the cellars of the Hôtel National des Invalides, shown here, to use against the Bastille later that day.

the crowd moved on to the Bastille, where they knew barrels of gunpowder were stored. At around 10 a.m., some 900 of them converged on the Bastille in Paris's eastern sector. This imposing fortress-prison had once housed political prisoners arrested by the monarchy and had come to be viewed as a hated symbol of the regime's past abuses. However, the structure's symbolic meaning was a secondary motive for targeting it. The gathered merchants, artisans, laborers, and soldiers (those French troops who had already defected to the revolutionary cause) were primarily interested in seizing the considerable stores of gunpowder held within.

At first, two representatives of the mob met with the fortress's governor (commander), Bernard-René Jordan de Launay. They demanded that he withdraw his cannons and allow the people to enter and collect the gunpowder they needed. If he agreed, there would be no need for bloodshed.

De Launay promised not to open fire on them; however, he did not allow them to collect the gunpowder.

While these negotiations were going on, the crowd became increasingly restless. Tempers flared, and the violence that all hoped to avoid erupted. The exact series of events that followed remains disputed because surviving eyewitness reports are somewhat contradictory, as each side claimed the other fired first. The following account by one of the officers stationed in the Bastille, though lacking in specific detail, is probably fairly accurate. He confirmed what all the accounts agree on, which is that de Launay eventually surrendered rather than risk the massacre of himself and his men:

> *[Members of the mob] cut the chains holding the drawbridge, and it fell open … After having easily dropped the bridge, they easily knocked down the door with axes and entered into the courtyard … I stationed my men to the left of the gate … I waited for the moment when the governor [was] to [act] and I was very surprised to see him send four veterans to the gates to open them and to lower the bridges. The crowd entered right away and disarmed us in an instant … In the castle, archives were thrown from the windows and everything was pillaged.*[33]

The brief, but momentous, battle resulted in hundreds dead, along with several wounded. Afterward, angry Parisians, convinced that de Launay had fired first, dragged him through the streets and killed him.

Although the battle was a small-scale one, the Bastille's fall had an enormous impact on the unfolding crisis. (Ever since, the French have celebrated July 14 as their independence day.) Put simply, Paris had fallen completely into the hands of the revolutionaries, and the power of the National Assembly was reinforced. King Louis had enough troops to storm and retake the city, but at what cost would this be accomplished? This was a question that echoed far and wide, including through the ranks of those troops. The king's officers soberly advised him that if he gave the order for the soldiers to fire on their fellow citizens, it would likely be disobeyed. William Doyle explained the meaning of this crucial turning point:

> *Louis XVI's acceptance of that advice marked the end of royal authority. The monarch recognized that he no longer had the power to enforce his will. He was therefore compelled finally to accept all that had been done since mid-June. The Estates-General had gone. They had been replaced by a single National Assembly … claiming sovereignty in the name of the nation and a mission to endow France with a constitution.*[34]

This engraving shows the storming of the Bastille on July 14, 1789.

Accordingly, with a mixture of reluctance and resignation, the king ordered his troops to withdraw.

Grande Peur

Though significant, this triumph of the people over the monarchy did not mark the end of the Revolution. Instead, it proved to be merely the end of the beginning of a long, sometimes violent national transformation. Indeed, the next round of turmoil began almost immediately. When news of the events in Paris filtered into the countryside, large portions of the nation were drawn into the unfolding drama. Rumors spread from one village and town to another. One quite incorrectly claimed that the king had ordered his troops into rural areas to suppress dissent among the peasants.

As a result, mass hysteria took hold in many areas. It became known as the *Grande Peur*, or "Great Fear," and lasted for almost three weeks. Tens of thousands of peasants armed

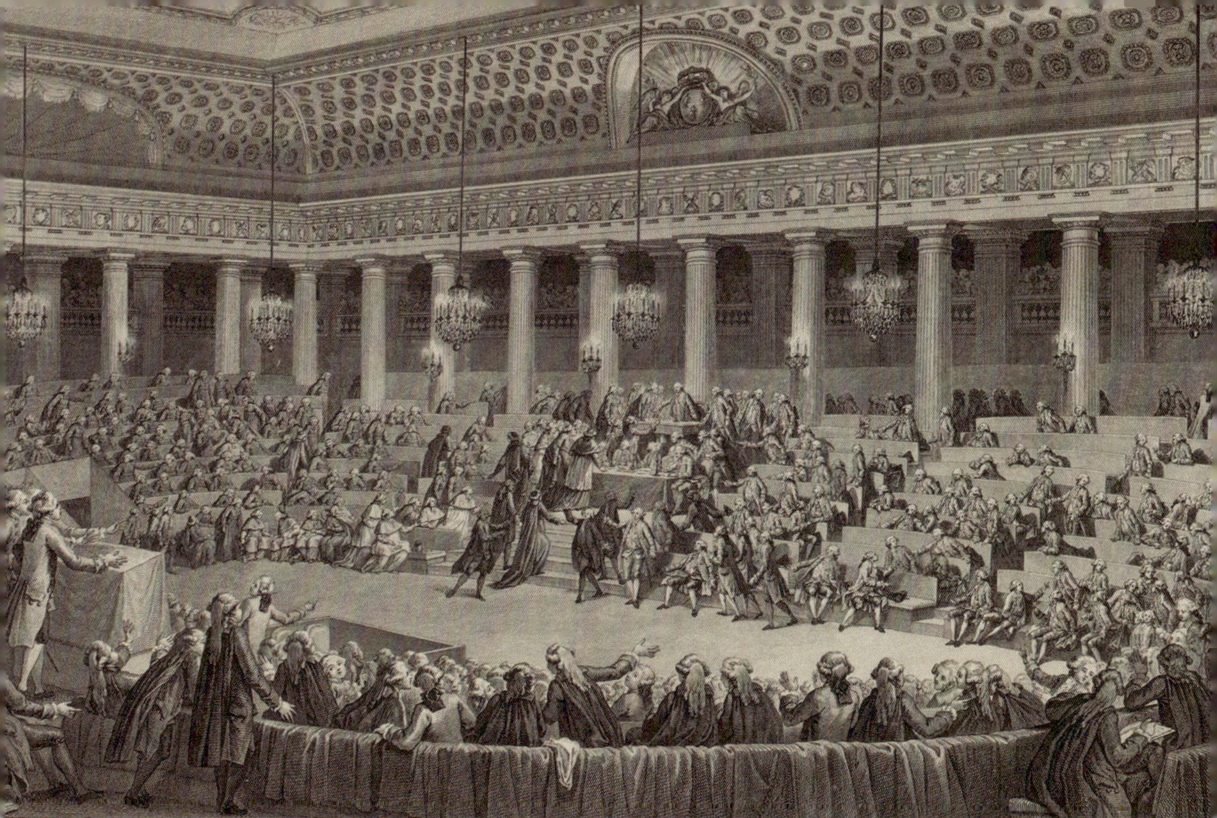

On the night of August 4, 1789, the National Assembly abolished feudalism and declared universal equality under the law at a meeting that is shown here.

themselves with whatever weapons they could find and barricaded themselves against the impending invasion. When it did not come, they went on a rampage. Their main targets were the chief symbols of the old feudal authority: the mansions of the rich lords who had long held so much power over the lives of millions. The marauders attacked, looted, and in some cases burned these wealthy manors after searching for food and drink.

More than anything, as one expert pointed out, they sought out the rooms where records were held. Destroying these feudal obligation records, the peasants reasoned, would deal a blow to the aristocrats' power to exploit them: "The rooms were ransacked, their contents burned, and distantly glimpsed smoke palls from bonfires of legal papers made their own contributions to the general panic."[35]

The nobles sitting in the National Assembly in Paris were appalled and frightened by the chaos in the countryside and became determined to stop it. In a dramatic gesture on the evening of August 4, all the aristocrats in the National Assembly renounced their own feudal rights,

THE END OF FEUDALISM

On August 4, 1789, the National Assembly abolished the feudal rights and privileges the nobles had long enjoyed. Their decree reads in part:

> *Feudal rights and dues deriving from real or personal* mainmorte *[a peasant's property that at his death passed to his noble lord] and personal servitude, and those representative thereof, are abolished ... The exclusive right of hunting and open warrens is likewise abolished; and every proprietor [landowner] has the right to destroy ... on his property only, every kind of game ... All [feudal] courts of justice are suppressed ... Tithes [taxes to support the Church] of every kind and dues which take the place thereof are abolished ... All citizens may be admitted, without distinction of birth, to all [religious], civil, and military employments and offices.*[1]

1. Quoted in John H. Stewart, ed., *A Documentary Survey of the French Revolution*. New York, NY: Macmillan, 1971, p. 107.

as well as all ancient feudal rights in France.

Trophime-Gérard, Marquis de Lally-Tollendal, an exasperated conservative, passed a message to the presiding deputy, pleading, "Suspend the session. They have all gone quite mad."[36]

Then, carried away by a spirit of justice and fairness for all, the legislators went on to remove other existing barriers among the social classes. "All citizens may be admitted, without distinction of birth, to all [religious], civil, and military employments and offices,"[37] one provision stated. This meant that all French male citizens were now equal under the law.

In retrospect, it is clear that the work of the National Assembly that night averted much loss of life and property. When word of the new, enlightened laws reached the countryside, the rioting subsided. The members of the National Assembly now turned their attention to what seemed to them the most important act: creating the new constitution for the country.

CHAPTER FOUR

SPONTANEOUS AND CALCULATED BLOODSHED

Coinciding with the fall of the Bastille and the events of August 4, 1789, the Constitutional Committee of the National Assembly began drafting France's first constitution and working to establish a constitutional monarchy. However, as students of the Enlightenment, they agreed that the first step in this process must be a declaration of universal rights. Enlightenment theorists raised the idea of thinking of society as being made up of individuals, each of whom was born with individual natural rights.

Further, they believed these rights should be similar in spirit and scope to those stated in Virginia's Declaration of Rights, written by George Mason in 1776, which listed not only universal rights but also individual rights, and the American Declaration of Independence, written by Thomas Jefferson in the same year. Many of the French watched closely as the Americans built a new government and nation, taking Enlightenment theory out of the books and putting it into practice.

The National Assembly soon completed both the declaration of rights and, within a couple of years, the new constitution. However, these documents turned out to be forged in blood. Though their authors were well-meaning and their provisions enlightened, neither the deputies nor their noble ideals could prevent continued outbreaks of violence. Some bloodshed, including massacres of innocent people, was spontaneous, but other bloodshed, including the brutal execution of the king, was coldly planned and carried out.

A Recognition of Human Freedoms

At first, the deputies of the National Assembly had no intention of resorting to or condoning violence. In fact, most of them assumed that the Bastille's fall in July and the following riots in the countryside represented the last blood that would be shed in the Revolution. Indeed, there seemed to be no need for further unrest. After all, the National Assembly was hard at work on a document that would address the fundamental rights of all French people. There was an optimistic feeling among the deputies that most citizens would see it as the beginning of a new era of peace and brotherhood.

The Declaration of the Rights of Man and of the Citizen was adopted on August 26, 1789, by the National Assembly as the first step toward writing a constitution for the Republic of France.

For models for their declaration of rights, the deputies had the American documents that the French legislators deeply admired. However, they wanted the French version to be even more sweeping in its recognition of human freedoms. One member of the National Assembly remarked that the Americans "have set a great example in the new hemisphere. Let us give one to the universe!"[38]

The document was adopted on August 26, 1789. Titled the Declaration of the Rights of Man and of the Citizen, it begins with these stirring words:

> *The representatives of the French people ... considering that ignorance, forgetfulness, or contempt of the rights of man are the sole causes of public miseries and the corruption of governments, have resolved to set forth in a solemn declaration the natural, inalienable, and sacred rights of man ... in order that the demands of the citizens ... may always take the direction of maintaining the constitution and welfare of all.*[39]

The document goes on to list basic civil rights, each based to one degree or another on the sentiments of the same Enlightenment thinkers who had inspired the American founding fathers. Like the American Bill of Rights, the French version established specific civil liberties, including the right to freedom from arbitrary arrest, equality of all citizens under the law, freedom of religion, and freedom of speech. The article guaranteeing the latter reads: "The free communication of ideas and opinions is one of the most precious of the rights of man. Every citizen can then freely speak, write, and print, subject to responsibility for the abuse of this freedom in the cases determined by law."[40]

In a surprisingly short amount of time, the French legislators created a statement of democratic principles that turned France's centuries-old system of absolute monarchy on its head. The inherited rights of a few privileged aristocrats were no longer meaningful or usable. In their place, the authors of the declaration substituted the notion that, as scholar Lynn Hunt wrote,

> *The legitimacy of government must flow from the guarantee of individual rights by the law. Under the monarchy, legitimacy depended on the king's will and his maintenance of a historic order that granted privileges according to rank and status. Most remarkably, the deputies of 1789 endeavored to make a statement of universal application, rather than one particularly or uniquely French, and it is that universality that has ensured the continuing resonance of the document.*[41]

Trouble at Versailles

Despite their democratic zeal, the vast majority of the National Assembly's deputies still did not plan to create a democracy like that of the United States. Rather, the French leaders expected that the new rights they had proposed would work within the framework of a constitutional monarchy. In that system, the king would still be the ceremonial head of state, and one of his duties would be to authorize the National Assembly's major legislation.

For these reasons, the deputies wanted King Louis to provide his official approval of the Declaration of the Rights of Man and of the Citizen. Thus, they presented the document to him in October. To their disappointment, however, he told them that he needed time to look it over in detail and that he would render his opinion on the matter later. How much later, the legislators wondered? Some deputies, as well as many other French, worried that the king might be stalling for a sinister reason. Perhaps, they suspected, he was planning to mobilize the army once again in a desperate bid to reinstate

On October 5, 1789, thousands of Parisian women met in the streets of Paris and marched in the rain to Louis's palace at Versailles.

his former powers.

Motivated by such concerns, and angry over continued bread shortages, one part of the population took action. On October 5, thousands of women gathered in the streets of Paris, armed with brooms, muskets, and pikes, and marched in the rain to Versailles. First, they demanded that the king use his wealth and influence to provide bread for hungry families. They also said they were there to support the Revolution and its principles. They had heard that the king's officers had made insulting remarks about the Revolution, and demanded that these officers be punished. Furthermore, the women asserted, in the future, the royal guards should be drawn solely from Parisian soldiers loyal to the Revolution.

Worried that the assembled women might become violent and hurt his family, King Louis gave in. He agreed to provide bread and approved the National Assembly's decrees and demands. The women did not trust him, however, and refused to take him at his word. They forced him and his family to move to the old Tuileries Palace in Paris, where they could keep a closer eye on his activities. The queen's foster brother, Joseph Weber, witnessed the march back to Paris and later described "the horror of a cold, somber, rainy day; the infamous militia splattering through the mud;

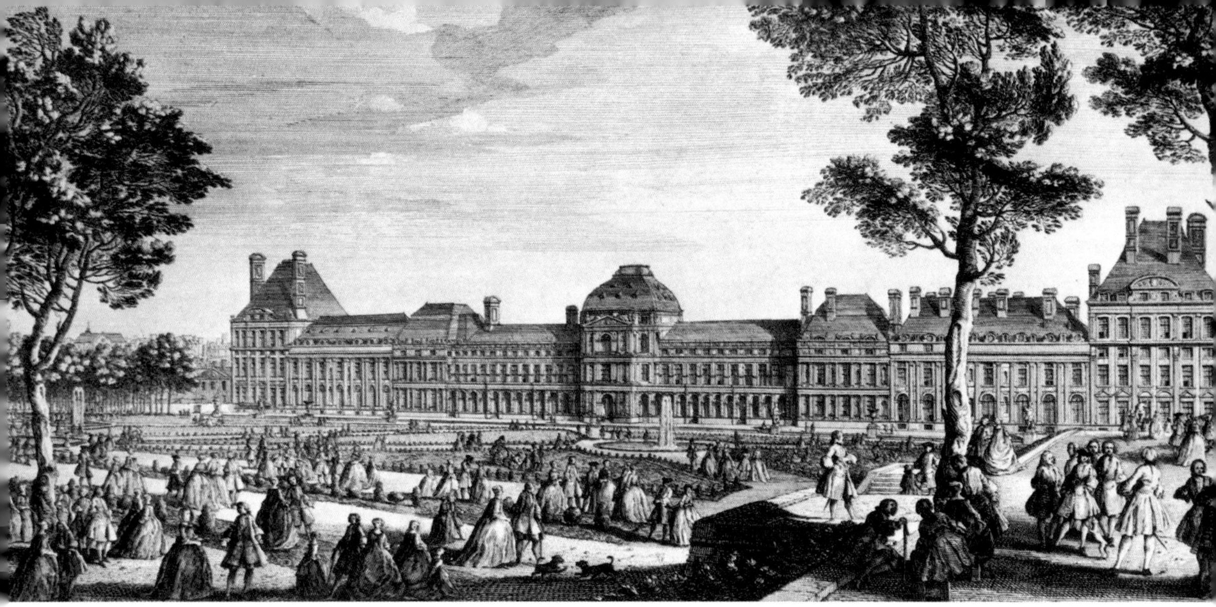

The women of Paris marched the king and his family to Tuileries Palace in Paris, shown here in the years before the Revolution.

the harpies, monsters with human faces; the captive monarch and his family … dragged along surrounded by guards."[42]

Reactions to the New Constitution

The king and his family remained under what amounted to house arrest for many months as the National Assembly's deputies worked diligently to finish writing the new constitution. That document affirmed that France would be a constitutional monarchy in which the king would be the head of state. However, he would essentially have to do the bidding of the national legislature, which would hold most of the real government authority.

The National Assembly also abolished the ancient French provinces. In their place, it created 83 local areas of roughly equal size called departments. Each department was subdivided into smaller units, including districts, cantons, and communes.

In addition, those drawing up the new constitution addressed many of the democratic concepts outlined in the Declaration of the Rights of Man and of the Citizen. For instance, they discussed the process of granting religious freedom to people of all faiths in the country. Particularly controversial in this regard was the situation of French Jews. The deputies had no argument with the idea of giving religious freedom to all citizens. The problem was that historically, the Jews, widely hated by Christians across Europe at the time, had never been considered true or complete French citizens. On January 28, 1790, a group of leading Jews presented the

National Assembly with the "Petition of Jews of Paris, Alsace, and Lorraine." It argued that Jews were legitimate citizens and should be granted the same rights as Catholics and Protestants:

> *The time has passed when one could say that it was only the dominant religion that could grant access to advantages [and] the lucrative and honorable posts in society. For a long time … the Protestants had no civil standing in France. Today, they [are] reestablished in the possession of this status. They are assimilated to the Catholics in everything … Why [not] the Jews? In general, civil rights are entirely independent from religious principles. And all men of whatever religion … we say, equally able to serve the fatherland, defend its interests, [and] contribute to its splendor, should all equally have the title and the rights of citizen.*[43]

Regardless of this reasoned argument, the deputies did not grant the Jews religious freedom in the constitution's initial draft. French Jews were not granted citizenship and full rights until September 1791.

Night Flight

The Jews were not the only French who were disappointed by the new constitution and the political system it had

ARGUMENT AGAINST EXECUTION

Shortly before King Louis XVI was executed in January 1793, numerous deputies wrote pamphlets or made speeches that were either for or against taking this step. One of the few pamphlets against his execution, excerpted here, was by Charles-François-Gabriel Morisson:

> *In the name of France, hear me out in silence, however shocking some of my reflections may appear. Citizens, like you I am overcome with the greatest indignation when I consider the many crimes, the atrocities, with which Louis XVI is stained. My first and doubtless most natural impulse is to see this bloody monster [be tormented and killed]. Yet … I must deny my impulse, and heed instead the voice of Reason [and] consult the spirit and disposition of our law … The Convention abolished the monarchy. From that moment, Louis had ceased to be king in law … Here, the National Convention … has nothing more to decide, since, by his de facto deposition [dethronement] he has already undergone the only punishment determined for those crimes which he committed while he was yet king.*[1]

1. Quoted in Michael Walzer, ed., *Regicide and Revolution: Speeches at the Trial of Louis XVI*. trans. Marian Rothstein. Cambridge, UK: Cambridge University Press, 1974, pp. 110, 120.

created. Most of the wealthiest nobles were disgruntled over the loss of their privileges, and a number of them fled to neighboring countries. There, they began inciting a counterrevolution that they hoped would restore France to its former state. They were called émigrés, from the French for "emigrants."

On the night of June 20, 1791, the king and his family disguised themselves as servants and set out toward France's northeastern border. However, the revolutionary authorities discovered what was happening. They caught up to the royals in Varennes and took them back to Paris, where an angry mob denounced King Louis as a traitor.

Charles-Philippe, comte d'Artois, younger brother of Louis XVI, as an exile in Germany, prepared for a counterrevolutionary invasion of France. A letter from Marie-Antoinette postponed it until after the royal family had escaped from Paris—an escape that never happened.

The king's attempted flight did much more than make him more unpopular than ever with the people. The incident also proved to be a difficult political situation that divided many of the revolutionaries. Scholars Laura Mason and Tracey Rizzo explained:

> *By fleeing, Louis undermined his image as a monarch loyal to the Revolution ... He encouraged counter-revolution, for opponents within and outside France could and did claim that the king was being held captive by a Revolution of which he wanted no part ... Perhaps most dangerously, the revolutionaries themselves had been divided ... Henceforth there would be two visible parties of revolution—those who would cling to the constitutional monarchy ... and those who would press with growing resistance for a republic and were willing to call on the crowd to achieve it.*[44]

Thus, the cause of French constitutional monarchy was already weakened when the National Assembly finished drafting the constitution in September 1791. On September 30, that body disbanded itself to make way for the new Legislative Assembly created in that document. The new legislature was indeed more anti-monarchy than the old one. The radical wing of the Legislative Assembly was a political club known as the Jacobins. (The club held meetings in a Dominican monastery library in Paris and adopted their nickname from the location.) They were intent on finding and crushing all counterrevolutionary forces and replacing the constitutional monarchy with a democratic republic. An even more radical faction within the Jacobins was named the Montagnards, ("mountain people" in French), and they were more extreme and uncompromising. Maximilien Robespierre and Georges Danton were part of the this faction.

Jacobins who were not Montagnards were called Girondins. They were only moderately radical and fairly open to discussion and compromise. Initially, the Girondins had control of the Legislative Assembly. One of their first official acts was to demand that all émigrés return to France at once or else forfeit their property, to which there was no response. Therefore, on April 20, 1792, the Legislative Assembly declared war on Austria, where many of the counterrevolutionary émigrés had settled. (Austria was also Marie-Antoinette's homeland.) Austria's ally, Prussia, then entered the war against France.

The onset of the war made many French more fearful and open to committing radical and violent acts in the name of patriotism. In September, when a Prussian general threatened to

Louis XVI and his family, dressed in disguise, were captured in Varennes as they attempted to escape from France.

Between September 2 and 7, 1792, a mob of angry men stormed several prisons in Paris and slaughtered as many as 1,400 prisoners.

destroy Paris, an angry mob, goaded by the incendiary words of journalist Jean-Paul Marat, took up arms against a population of prisoners whom they believed were trying to betray them. In the words of historian David Andress, it was believed they "could, at a moment's notice, be broken out and armed by the still-active cells of the hydra-headed counter-revolution."[45] This band of misguided, angry men proceeded to storm three prisons in Paris: the Châtelet, the Conciergerie, and La Force. The following morning they moved on to two temporary prisons and in the afternoon, death came to the prisoners at Bicêtre. On the fourth day, the men stormed and slaughtered the prisoners in the women's hospital-prison of La Salpêtrière. As many as 1,400 prisoners were massacred in the killing spree.

The Rise of the Sansculottes

This was not the end of what many French came to see as senseless violence. Eventually, the extreme Jacobins, the Montagnards, joined forces with a group of dissatisfied Parisian shopkeepers, artisans, and factory workers called the sansculottes. (The

PRO-WAR RHETORIC

In January 1792, deputies hotly debated whether to go to war with Austria. This is an excerpt from a pro-war speech made by Jacques-Pierre Brissot:

> *It is necessary to make war now. We are sure of success in being the first to attack. All the advantages await us on enemy territory. All the disasters will follow us in our homes. Furthermore, gentlemen, all that can be said on this question can be reduced to this. [Either] the emperor [of Austria] wants war, or he only wants it in the spring, or he does not want it at all. If he wants it, it is necessary [for us to attack first]. If he only wants it next spring, it is still necessary to hasten to prevent him. If he does not want it at all, it is necessary to force him to [fight]. Therefore, in each case war is necessary.*[1]

1. Quoted in Laura Mason and Tracey Rizzo, *The French Revolution: A Document Collection*. Boston, MA: Houghton Mifflin, 1999, p. 164.

Jacques-Pierre Brissot, a leading member of the Girondins, argued for war with Austria in 1792.

term means "without breeches," a reference to the silk knee breeches worn by the nobility and bourgeoisie. Working class men wore *pantalons*, which were long trousers.) The members of this new coalition were galvanized into radical action partly by the impending threat of the advancing Prussian army. On September 20, 1792, they created a legislative body they called the National Convention and proclaimed France to be a Republic.

Implicit in the definition of "republic" was the fact that the monarchy was now outdated and invalid. Moreover, the very presence of the monarch and his royal relatives made the new radical leaders feel uncomfortable, even

"IT WOUNDS MY HEART ..."

King Louis XVI delivered his last public speech on December 26, 1792, at the end of his trial. He said in part:

Speaking to you perhaps for the last time, I declare to you that my conscience does not reproach me in any way and that my defenders have told you nothing but the truth. I have never feared a public examination of my conduct. But it wounds my heart to find in the indictment the charge that I wished to shed the people's blood ... I confess that the often repeated pledges that I have at all times given of my love for the people and the way in which I have always behaved seem to me an evident proof that I had little fear of endangering myself in order to spare their blood, and that these pledges and this behavior should preserve me forever from any such [accusation].[1]

1. Quoted in Bernard Fay, *Louis XVI; or, The End of the World*. trans. Patrick O'Brian. Chicago, IL: Henry Regnery, 1968, p. 397.

humiliated. "The king was there," scholars Norah Lofts and Margery Weiner wrote, "alive in the prison." He was "an anachronism," (something that doesn't belong in this time) and "an embarrassing one."[46]

The sansculottes, shown here, represented the lower classes in French society.

The radical leaders of the National Convention decided, therefore, that getting rid of King Louis would be best for all. However, no one was willing to go so far as to kill him without a trial, which was an act that might turn the people against the National Convention. With that in mind, they proceeded to put

The former king was put on trial by the National Convention and sentenced to death.

the king on trial in December 1792. "The king made a poor appearance," Lofts and Weiner continued:

> *Denied the use of a razor for three days, he wore the beginning of a beard on cheeks that now sagged flabbily. His brown coat was shabby. [But] there still clung about him the ghost, the vanishing shadow of royalty. He had been allowed counsel to defend him, [but] against what? For being born to the throne? Being passive? Being stupid? When the prosecution declared, "Louis, the French nation is your accuser," the impersonal nature of the trial was revealed. It was not Louis who was on trial; it was the system of monarchy.*[47]

The Girondins, now a minority in the legislature, tried but failed to save the king's life. He was sentenced to death and beheaded in a bloody public spectacle on January 21, 1793. Many of the legislators, along with other French, hoped that the bloodshed was over at last. However, they were wrong; the worst was yet to come.

Chapter Five

REVOLUTION IN CRISIS

According to historian Peter McPhee, "There are few crises in modern history comparable to that summer of 1793, when a revolutionary nation wracked by civil war and dissent was evidently about to be overrun by a coalition of its neighbors."[48] R. R. Palmer added:

> *Anarchy within, invasion from without. A country cracking from outside pressure, disintegrating from internal strain. Revolution is at its height. War. Inflation. Hunger. Fear. Hate. Sabotage. Fanaticism. Hopes. Boundless idealism … and the dread that all the gains of the Revolution would be lost. And the faith that if they won, they would bring Liberty, Equality, Fraternity to the world.*[49]

The leaders of the National Convention in Paris struggled to hold the Revolution together against a number of problems and threats, including the plots that the French émigrés continued to hatch against it from abroad and federalists who wanted local power rather than national power and who seemed set on destroying the republic in the name of the republic. They had to face uprisings of rural peasants who did not want to fight in the war, a national economy in shambles because of all the civil and social unrest, and the unpredictable Paris mob, which various political factions might at any moment sway against the Revolution's leaders. Although the National Convention was successful in completing a constitution and holding a successful national referendum on it, the climate in the country made it impossible to implement it just yet.

Collectively, many leaders felt these difficulties and dangers foreshadowed the Revolution's collapse and France's descent into chaos. In the view of the more radical deputies, the only realistic way to prevent such a catastrophe was to crack down on any and all who threatened the ideals and implementation of the Revolutionary government. In a speech to the National Convention, Maximilien Robespierre justified using force to preserve liberty:

> *It has been said that terror was the mainspring of despotic government. Does your government, then, resemble a despotism? Yes, as the sword which glitters in the hands of liberty's heroes resembles the one with which tyranny's lackeys are armed. Let the despot govern his brutalized subjects by terror; he is right to do this, as a despot. Subdue liberty's enemies by terror, and you will be right, as founders of the Republic. The government of the revolution is the despotism of liberty against tyranny. Is force made only to protect crime? And is it not to strike the heads of the proud that lightning is destined? Nature imposes upon every physical and moral being the law of providing for its own preservation. Crime slaughters innocence in order to reign, and innocence in the hands of crime fights with all its strength.*[50]

In the name of liberty, therefore, Robespierre and his colleagues instituted what came to be known as the Reign of Terror, which lasted from September 1793 to late July 1794. It enforced its authority through a series of revolutionary decrees and tribunals (committees, hearings, and trials) in which enemies of the new republic were arrested and, in many cases, executed. The exact number of victims remains unclear. However, at least 300,000 people were arrested, and as many as 40,000 lost their lives—at least 17,000 in Paris alone. Eventually, this fury of

The guillotine was used extensively during the Reign of Terror.

Shown here is a portrait of Maximilien Robespierre, who was one of the architects of the Reign of Terror.

suspicion, deceit, paranoia, and violence could no longer sustain itself. Even its leaders came to be seen as suspects, and as they turned on one another, the Reign of Terror began to destroy itself.

Terror Is the Order of the Day

It is possible that the Reign of Terror would never have occurred if France had been at peace in 1793. However, as that year began, the French were already at war with Austria and Prussia (in what is now called the War of the First Coalition). Then, when Louis XVI was executed on January 21, shocked heads of state across Europe expressed their outrage by expelling their French ambassadors. In response, the National Convention in Paris declared war on Britain, Holland, and Spain. Soon Revolutionary France stood alone against nearly every major European power. Other European nations, even the few not at war with France, feared the outbreak of similar rebellions in their own countries, so most of them instituted highly repressive domestic policies. Early in 1793, for example, British leaders attempted to censor the press. In Russia, Catherine the Great burned the works of popular French philosophers, including Voltaire, and exiled freedom-minded Russian writers to Siberia.

Robespierre, Danton, and the other leaders of the Montagnards, who now headed France's government, at first felt confident that France could achieve victory in the war. For one thing, they reasoned, the country had a large population from which to draw soldiers. They took advantage of that fact when, in the spring of 1793, the National Convention drafted virtually everyone in France into some sort of military service. "The French people are in permanent requisition for army service," the *lévee en masse* stated. "The young men shall go to battle. The married men shall forge

THE GUILLOTINE

Many of the executions carried out during the Revolution utilized the guillotine, which was a device that had a huge blade that fell vertically and sliced off the victim's head. It was named for Joseph-Ignace Guillotin, a Paris physician who told the Legislative Assembly that it would be a swift and less painful form of execution for people of all social classes. Similar devices had already been used in England, Scotland, and elsewhere for more than a century. However, the Legislative Assembly's deputies ordered that a French version be constructed by a German engineer following a design by Dr. Antoine Louis, the Secretary of the Academy of Surgery. For this reason, the device was briefly referred to as the "Louisette," after Dr. Louis. The first use of the term "guillotine" occurred shortly after the first execution in 1792.

This painting shows an execution by guillotine during the Reign of Terror that lasted nearly a year.

arms and transport provisions. The women shall make tents and clothes and shall serve in the hospitals. The children shall turn old linen into lint [for use in muskets] ... National buildings shall be converted into barracks [and] public places into armament workshops."[51]

Another reason that France's revolutionary leaders were certain of victory was their steadfast belief in their cause. They were sure that the French, as champions of human freedom, were destined to prevail over the forces of monarchy and oppression. They expressed this belief by having all French battle banners inscribed with the words: "The French people have risen against tyrants."

In addition to overseeing the national effort to fight the forces of the First Coalition, the National Convention's deputies faced an equally daunting task. Namely, they had to govern and stabilize a large nation still filled with opposing political groups and unrest. To confront this challenge, Montagnard leaders formed a series of committees, which were groups of men charged with individual, targeted goals.

The most important and powerful of these groups, the Committee of Public Safety, rapidly assumed nearly complete governmental authority. Its radical members, especially Robespierre, Danton, Louis-Antoine Saint-Just, and Lazare Carnot, became powerful and widely feared. Another fanatic, the journalist Jean-Paul Marat, who helped instigate the September massacres by his provocative language, agreed with and aided Robespierre and the other members of the Committee. They even profited by Marat's untimely and brutal death. In July 1793, he was fatally stabbed in his bathtub by Charlotte Corday, a young woman of federalist tendencies who feared that Marat was on track to destroy her beloved Republic. In the days before her execution, she stated that she was always a Republican, even before the Revolution. Because the Committee was critical of the Girondins, it promptly used the incident to associate her with that party and subsequently discredit them.

Other questionable tactics included the Committee's increasing use of undemocratic decrees, intimidation, and even brutality to achieve its idealistic aims. By September 1793, the Reign of Terror and dictatorship were in full swing. "This was not a dictatorship of any one particular member," a modern scholar pointed out, "but the committee certainly exercised the powers of a dictatorial regime."[52] Robespierre and his accomplices claimed they had no other choice. They faced an extreme national emergency, they said, and the use of force was the only means of restoring stability and safety. After this restoration, they promised, there would no longer be any need for suppressive measures. One popular Parisian newspaper accepted this argument and tried to

This image shows Charlotte Corday after she murdered Jean-Paul Marat in his bathtub.

sell it to its readers. "Yes, terror is the order of the day, and ought to be," an editorial began. It continued,

> *Is not the French Revolution [a battle] to the death between those who want to be free and those content to be slaves? This is the situation, and the French people have gone too far to retreat with honor and safety. There is no middle ground. France must be utterly free or perish in the attempt, and any means are justifiable in fighting for so fine a cause. But our resources are being exhausted, say some. Well, when the Revolution is finished, they will be replenished by peace.*[53]

The Penalty for All Offenses Is Death

The radical, ruthless men who now ran France needed powerful, effective tools to maintain and assert their dictatorial authority. One of these tools was the secretive, autocratic (having unlimited authority) structure and powers of the Committee of Public Safety itself. A decree issued in April 1793 outlined these powers:

> *This committee shall deliberate in secret. It shall be responsible for supervising and accelerating the work of [the revolutionary government], whose decrees it may even suspend when it believes them contrary to the national interest ... It is authorized to take, in urgent circumstances, measures for general defense, both internal and external, and its decrees ... shall be executed without delay.*[54]

Thus, when Robespierre and his fellow dictators felt that a decree passed by the National Convention was "contrary to the national interest," they could veto it. This was completely contrary to democratic principles. As in all dictatorships in recorded history, the "national interest" inevitably could not be separated from the personal interests of the dictators themselves.

Of course, the Committee's members justified their assumption of these powers by citing national security concerns. National security also became the excuse for the creation of a means for identifying the government's (and often the dictators') enemies. It took the form of the Law of Suspects, passed in September 1793, which read in part:

> *The following are deemed suspected persons: those who, by their conduct, associations, talk, or writings have shown themselves partisans of tyranny or federalism and enemies of liberty ... those to whom certificates of patriotism have been refused ... those former nobles, together with husbands, wives, fathers, mothers, sons or daughters ... and agents of the* émigrés, *who*

have not steadily manifested their devotion to the Revolution.[55]

Later, even more repressive measures were enacted, widening the net in which the members of the Committee hoped to ensnare their enemies. The most dictatorial of all was the Law of 22 Prairial Year II, passed on June 10, 1794. "The revolutionary tribunal is instituted in order to punish the enemies of the people," one article stated. It continued:

The enemies of the people are those who seek to destroy public liberty ... [those] who have [tried] to depreciate [criticize] the National Convention ... those who have deceived the people or the representatives of the people in order to lead them into operations contrary to the interests of liberty ... those who have spread false news in order to divide and disturb the people ... those who shall have sought to mislead opinion and to prevent the instruction of the people, to [corrupt the public's morals and conscience] ... and the purity of the revolutionary and republican principles.

The law also spelled out the punishment that awaited these enemies: "Every citizen has the right to seize and to arraign before the magistrates conspirators and counterrevolutionaries. He is required to denounce them when he knows of them."[56] The penalty for all offenses was death.

Definition of an Enemy

These documents demonstrate how the definition of an enemy of the people swiftly expanded, making more and more people and groups suspects. Having been empowered by the Committee's obsessive decrees, those in power engaged in a systematic slaughter of thousands of people. According to Christopher Hibbert:

Whole families were led to the scaffold for no other crime than their relationship; sisters for shedding tears over the death of their brothers in the emigrant armies; wives for lamenting the fate of their husbands ... Others were sentenced on the strength of denunciations by jealous or vindictive neighbors. One victim was fetched from prison to face a charge which had been brought against another prisoner with a similar name. Her protests were silenced by the prosecutor, who said casually, "Since she's here, we might just as well take her."[57]

The most famous of the Reign of Terror's victims were the former queen Marie-Antoinette, members of the royal family, and several other nobles. The queen had already suffered

The execution of Marie-Antoinette was a major public event. Many saw it as a triumph of the Revolution over the former monarchy.

greatly from the loss of her husband, her royal status, and her once luxurious lifestyle. However, this was not enough for the extremists now running the government. She was arrested, charged with treason and committing incest with her son, and held in a cell in the Conciergerie, a prison near Notre Dame Cathedral in Paris.

Marie-Antoinette's trial took place on October 14, 1793. When called to comment on the incest charge, which was almost certainly false, she replied: "If I give no answer, it is because nature itself refuses to accept such an accusation brought against a mother. I appeal to all the mothers here present."[58] These words elicited some sympathy from the spectators. Nevertheless, the judge threatened to clear the court and sped up the inevitable guilty verdict. Denied any right to appeal, she was executed two days later (October 16) in the same manner as her husband—beheaded in public by a guillotine.

Former aristocrats and suspected counterrevolutionaries were not the only victims of the Reign of Terror.

MARIE-ANTOINETTE IN PRISON

One of Marie-Antoinette's lawyers later recalled her situation in prison just prior to her trial:

On October 14th, 1793, I happened to be in the country when I received the news that I had been named ... to defend the Queen before the revolutionary tribunal ... I immediately set out for the prison filled with a sense of the sacred duty ... After passing through two gates one enters a dark corridor ... On the right are the cells, and on the left there is a chamber into which the light enters by two small barred windows looking onto the little courtyard reserved for women. It was in this chamber that the Queen was confined. It was divided into two parts by a screen. On the left ... was an armed [guard], and on the right the part of the room occupied by the Queen containing a bed, a table and two chairs. Her Majesty was attired in a white dress of extreme simplicity ... In presenting myself to the Queen with respectful devotion, I felt my knees trembling under me and my eyes wet with tears.[1]

1. Quoted in Georges Pernoud and Sabine Flaissier, eds., *The French Revolution.* trans. Richard Graves. New York, NY: Capricorn, 1961, pp. 203–204.

Before the Revolution, Marie-Antoinette was seen as a symbol of royal corruption and waste.

As time went on, its administrators became both suspicious and bold enough to eliminate fellow revolutionaries and National Convention deputies. Some were targeted for being too moderate. These included several Girondins who had urged the ruling group to use more caution and humanity. Others were arrested on false charges simply because Robespierre and his colleagues on the Committee did not like or trust them.

The Reign of Terror Falls Apart

Such injustices, which many viewed as a disgrace to the Revolution's original ideals, continued with increasing intensity until they ended in a shocking spectacle. Simply put, the Reign of Terror's principal leaders began to kill their own. Danton was the first to go. He had begun to see that many of the recent arrests had been unreasonable and had the nerve to say so in a speech delivered to the National Convention in late January 1794. "No one asked for revolutionary committees more than I," he declared. "They were necessary then. [However, we must] be wary ... Justice must be rendered in such a way that it will not weaken the strictness of our measures."[59]

For expressing such sentiments, Danton was arrested on March 30. After enduring a rigged trial with a predetermined outcome, he and another revolutionary seen as too moderate, Camille Desmoulins, were guillotined on April 5. Reportedly, Danton's last words were, "Show my head to the people. It is worth seeing."[60]

It soon became clear to most other members of the National Convention that, if Danton was not safe, no

Robespierre, Danton, and Marat are shown here having a heated discussion.

"LET US CRUSH THE ENEMIES OF THE REVOLUTION"

On September 5, 1793, the Convention in Paris voted in favor of the idea of using "terror," or necessary force, to destroy all enemies of the Revolution, be they real or potential. One deputy told those gathered:

> *Legislators, it is time to put an end to the impious struggle that has been going on since 1789 between the sons and daughters of the nation and those who have abandoned it. Your fate, and ours, is tied to the unvarying establishment of the republic. We must either destroy its enemies, or they will destroy us. They have thrown down the gauntlet in the midst of the People, who have picked it up. They have stirred up agitation. They have attempted to separate, to divide the mass of the citizens, in order to crush the People and to avoid being crushed themselves. Today, the mass of the People, who are without resources, must destroy them using their own weight and willpower … Let us crush the enemies of the revolution, and starting today, let the government take action, let the laws be executed, let the lot of the People be strengthened, and let liberty be saved.*[1]

1. Quoted in "Terror Is the Order of the Day," Liberty, Equality, Fraternity: Exploring the French Revolution. chnm.gmu.edu/revolution/d/416/.

one was, and eventually, the moderates gathered enough courage to challenge Robespierre and the remaining dictators. On July 27, 1794, cries of "Down with the tyrant!"[61] echoed throughout the hall as they publicly condemned him. They also denounced Saint-Just. The next day, these two men and 20 of their closest supporters felt the executioner's blade. For these overzealous revolutionaries, the wheel of justice had come full circle. Though the Reign of Terror was over, the larger Revolution had not yet expended its considerable energies.

CHAPTER SIX

REVOLUTIONARY CULTURE AND SOCIETY

As one radical document of 1793 proclaimed, "to be truly Republican, each citizen must experience and bring about in himself a revolution equal to the one which has changed France. There is nothing, absolutely nothing in common between the slave of a tyrant and the inhabitant of a free state; the customs of the latter, his principles, his sentiments, his action, all must be new."[62]

During the first half of the Revolution, French society and culture underwent a series of distinct changes. Since the main principles of political change wrought by these revolutionaries were equality, freedom, and the rights of individual citizens to control their government, it seemed only natural and correct that these same ideas should be applied to society. Thus, various assemblies pushed to rid society of those institutions and customs that denied or discouraged individual freedom of expression and a person's right to determine his or her own destiny.

The Catholic Church had long been one of the most powerful institutions in France and made up the First Estate. Its bishops and priests controlled many aspects of French society, life, and thought, including education and marriage customs. The Revolution's leaders felt that the Church had too much control and discouraged individual thought and expression. Therefore, they swiftly moved to place the churches under government control and limit the powers and privileges of the clergy. The most radical revolutionaries thought that did not go far enough, so they attempted to de-Christianize France and replace traditional religious beliefs with state-sponsored secular (nonreligious) beliefs.

Similarly, the state took over the Church's role in education by establishing public schools. Marriage customs were overhauled, and divorce was legalized.

The revolutionaries also decided to remake time itself by taking the Gregorian calendar and replacing it with a new republican one. After all, the old calendar began with the birth of Christ and marked out the year in the liturgical progression of religious holidays. They thought science and republican politics should structure time—not religion. The revolutionaries also established a national institute of arts and sciences and a new system of weights and measures, which was the metric system.

Some of these innovations and changes did not survive very long following the end of the Revolution. Also, the revolutionaries were not progressive enough in certain social areas; despite their idealism about equality, for instance, they refused to grant women the same political rights most men now enjoyed. Nevertheless, the Revolution had profound effects on French society and thought and, in many ways, paved the way for the emergence of modern secular French and European culture.

Theocracy versus Freedom of Conscience

Religious developments in France constitute a clear example of how the Revolution permanently altered the country's society and culture. The revolutionaries went after the Catholic Church for a number of reasons. First was the inequity of the special privileges enjoyed by the bishops who treated the commoners as inferiors. Among these privileges was exemption from paying taxes, which all commoners had to pay. Another religious custom the revolutionaries viewed as an abuse was the mandatory tithe. This was a proportion of each commoner's yearly income that he or she had to pay to help support the Church. Second, many also resented the high levels of corruption that existed among the bishops and the fact that the bishops always sided with the nobles against the commoners. "The 'good conscience' of 1789 wanted the Church to be purer [and] poorer," scholar Emmet Kennedy pointed out, "more responsive to the indigent [needy] and more removed from the [royal] court and aristocracy."[63]

The first assaults on the Church came in the Revolution's opening months. Among the feudal privileges the National Assembly abolished on August 4, 1789, was the tithe. This was a serious blow to the bishops, who had long counted on the tithe as one of their principal sources of income. The National Assembly struck the Church an even harsher blow on November 2. They voted and agreed to confiscate the vast lands owned by the clergy and place them at the

THE NEW CALENDAR

The French revolutionaries wanted to wipe out as many bad memories of the nation's past as they could, including the calendar and holidays that had been established by the Church and kings. In October 1793, members of a committee chosen to draw up a new calendar reported:

> *The main idea upon which we have based our proposal is to use the calendar to consecrate the agricultural system, to lead the nation back to it, highlighting periods and times of the year with clear or tangible signs taken from agriculture and the rural economy … We have therefore developed the idea of giving each month of the year a characteristic name that depicts its unique temperature and the types of agricultural produce in season at that time … Thus the names of the months are:*
>
> *AUTUMN*
> *Vendémiaire (Vintage)*
> *Brumaire (Fog)*
> *Frimaire (Frost)*
> *WINTER*
> *Nivôse (Snow)*
> *Pluviôse (Rain)*
> *Ventôse (Wind)*
> *SPRING*
> *Germinal (Buds)*
> *Floréal (Flowers)*
> *Prairial (Meadow)*
> *SUMMER*
> *Messidor (Harvest)*
> *Thermidor (Heat)*
> *Fructidor (Fruit)*[1]

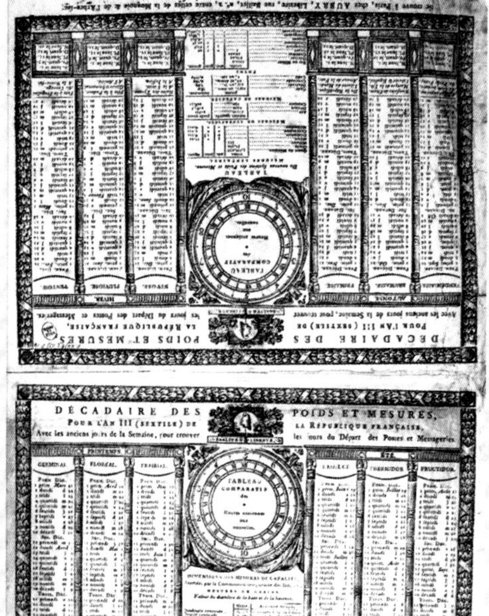

This is what the new Republican calendar based on nature looked like; the creators gave each month of the year a characteristic name that depicted its unique temperature and the types of agricultural produce in season at that time.

1. Quoted in "The Calendar," Liberty, Equality, Fraternity: Exploring the French Revolution. chnm.gmu.edu/revolution/d/435/.

disposal of the French people. The Church's authority was also undermined by Article 10 of the new Declaration of Rights, which reduced the clergy's strong influence over the way people thought and expressed themselves. "No one should be disturbed on account of his opinion, even religious [opinion],"[64] the article states.

These controversial moves proved to be only the start of more comprehensive ones in which the National Assembly made the Church nothing more than a part of the state and thereby subject to state rules. In July 1790, the deputies passed the Civil Constitution of the Clergy. It ordained that clergymen's salaries be paid by the state; reduced the number of bishops; matched up each diocese (church district) with one of the new geographic departments the National Assembly had recently created; and most controversial of all, mandated that priests and bishops be chosen by the people in free elections, rather than by church officials. Even more humiliating for clergymen was the demand that they recite an oath of loyalty to the state, as follows: "I swear to be faithful to the nation, to the law and the king, and to maintain with all my power the Constitution determined by the National Assembly and accepted by the king."[65] In spring of 1791, Pope Pius VI condemned these reforms.

De-Christianization of France

An even more vigorous assault on the Church came in late 1793 and early 1794 at the hands of the radical leaders of the committees enforcing the Reign of Terror. The goal was to de-Christianize France. As Christopher Hibbert wrote:

> *Religious monuments outside churches were destroyed. Various religious ceremonies were suppressed … Not only streets and squares but towns and villages [changed from religious to secular] names. The bestowal on babies of revolutionary first names became more common in certain districts than those of saints. More and more cathedrals and churches were deprived of their ornaments, vessels, and [gold] plate [and] some were converted into Temples of Reason. [Also] many clergy resigned and a number married.*[66]

In place of Christianity, the extremists tried to establish the "Cult of the Supreme Being." That Being, a Deist god—perhaps similar to the one considered by Thomas Jefferson, Benjamin Franklin, and several other American founding fathers—created the universe but thereafter did not intervene in human affairs. The Americans, however, believed in the separation of church and state, and would have opposed Robespierre's attempt to create a state religion.

A NEW SYSTEM OF MEASUREMENT

Among the many cultural changes initiated by the revolutionaries was the introduction of the metric system for weights and measures, which was simpler and more uniform than the many conflicting systems that then existed in Europe. An April 1795 decree stated in part:

> *There is only one standard of weights and measures for the entire Republic; there shall be a platinum ruler on which will be marked the meter, which has been adopted as the fundamental unit of the whole system of measurement … Henceforth the new measures shall be [called]:*
>
> *Meter, the measure equal to one-ten millionth of the arc of the terrestrial meridian included between the north pole and the equator;*
>
> *Acre, The measure of area for land, equal to a square, ten meters to a side …*
>
> *Liter, the measure of volume, both for liquids and for dry material, the capacity of which shall be the cube of one-tenth of a meter;*
>
> *Gram, the absolute weight of a volume of pure water equal to the cube of one one-hundredth of a meter, at the temperature of melting ice.*
>
> *Finally the monetary unit shall take the name of [the] franc.*[1]

1. Quoted in John H. Stewart, ed., *A Documentary Survey of the French Revolution*. New York, NY: Macmillan, 1971, pp. 555–556.

In the summer of 1794, Robespierre founded the annual Festival of the Supreme Being, saying in part:

> *The eternally happy day which the French people consecrate to the Supreme Being has finally arrived. Never has the world he created offered him a sight so worthy of his eyes. He has seen tyranny, crime, and deception reign on earth. At this moment, he sees an entire nation, at war with all the oppressors of the human race, suspend its heroic efforts in order to raise its thoughts and vows to the Great Being who gave it the mission to undertake these efforts and the strength to execute them.*[67]

Not surprisingly, angry Catholic reactions soon set in against the various attacks on the Church. Many French, faced with choosing between patriotism and religion, found themselves in a crisis of conscience. Tens of thousands demanded that their churches be reopened and decorations and other church items that had been removed be returned. Some people even worried that various local natural disasters that occurred each year might be God's punishment for the Revolution's anti-Christian policies.

Christianity was too ingrained in French society to be eradicated by a few government edicts and programs. As a result, in the years following the Revolutionary era, the Catholic Church rebounded. Still, it recovered only a fraction of the power and influence it had possessed before the Revolution. Having been humbled in the people's eyes, thereafter the clergy was obliged to cater more to the needs of its church members.

Education Reform

Reorganizing the Church necessarily resulted in other reforms, among them a new school system. Before the French Revolution, education had been primarily in the hands of the clergy. Classes were held mainly in parish halls, taught by priests, restricted to children of the upper and middle classes, and paid for by the students' parents. The Enlightenment concepts that had inspired the Revolution (such as equality and democratic principles) were largely excluded from the curriculum.

In secularizing church activities, the revolutionaries dismantled the old schools. The new system they created featured both primary and secondary (high school) education regulated by the government and open to all children, an approach later adopted in all modern Western societies. The Jacobins and other revolutionaries saw two major goals of the new schools: First, they would provide young citizens basic skills that would give them all an equal chance in life; second, they would indoctrinate children in

Marie-Jean-Antoine-Nicolas de Caritat, marquis de Condorcet, was a prominent French intellectual who advocated for robust education reform.

SUBORDINATION ENCOURAGED

One of the major literary works of the European Enlightenment, the *Encyclopédie* (edited by leading intellectual Denis Diderot and published between 1751 and 1772), included the following in its article about women, reflecting the thinking of that time:

> *Even though husband and wife have the same fundamental interests in society, it is nevertheless essential that governmental authority rests with either one or the other. The positive rights of civilized nations, like the laws and customs of Europe, now grant this authority unanimously and definitively to the male, who, being gifted with greater strength of mind and body, contributes more to the common good in matters both human and holy. Women then, must necessarily be subordinate to their husbands and obey his orders on all household issues. These are the opinions of legal advisors, both in olden times and now, as well as the unequivocal decision of legislators.*[1]

1. Quoted in "Article from the Encyclopedia: 'Woman'," Liberty, Equality, Fraternity: Exploring the French Revolution. chnm.gmu.edu/revolution/d/469/.

the Revolution's ideals, thereby helping to continue the new, fairer revolutionary society. In a report to the legislators, noted French intellectual Marie-Jean-Antoine-Nicolas de Caritat, marquis de Condorcet, summarized the new system's ambitious aims: "Education must be universal [and] extend to all citizens. [Also] it must, in its several degrees, comprise the entire system of human knowledge, and assure to men of all ages the facility of preserving their knowledge or of acquiring new knowledge."[68] Condorcet was also a proponent of the rights of women, but his proposal for education reform was more successful.

To these ends, in 1794, the National Convention enacted a system of primary schools for all French boys and girls. The legislation reads in part:

> *The primary schools shall be distributed throughout the territory of the Republic in proportion to population; accordingly, there shall be one primary school for every 1,000 inhabitants ...*
>
> *Each primary school shall be divided into two sections, one for boys and one for girls; accordingly, there shall be one man teacher and one woman teacher ...*
>
> *The teachers shall be chosen by the*

people; nevertheless, throughout the duration of the Revolutionary Government, they shall be examined, selected, and supervised by a jury of instruction, composed of three [local government officials].[69]

In addition to their selection by the people, the teachers were paid by the state. The state also mandated the curriculum, which included instruction in reading and writing; the new Declaration of Rights and constitution; morality (as defined by the revolutionaries); French language; geography and natural phenomena (science); heroic national songs; and daily physical exercise.

The National Convention also set up secondary schools, equivalent to modern high schools. There was a "central school" located in each of the new departments. In addition, the government established college-like institutions that included a school of public works (which, in the 20th century, became one of the finest technical schools in the world), an early version of a teachers' college, three medical colleges, and the National Institute, which offered classes in science, mathematics, philosophy, literature, and the arts.

Women in Revolutionary France

Education turned out to be the main area of advancement for French women during the Revolution. The vast majority of men, including the radical revolutionaries, and most women, too, accepted traditional views of women and their societal roles. Both before and during the Revolution, many French women worked as farmers, laundresses, and shopkeepers. Most were also wives and mothers and, due partially to Church doctrine, they felt these were their chief roles. The ideal woman was summarized by a Jacobin journalist, who gave this advice in 1793:

> *Be honest and diligent girls, tender and modest wives, wise mothers, and you will be good patriots. True patriotism consists of fulfilling one's duties and valuing only rights appropriate to each according to sex and age, and not wearing the [liberty] cap [and] not carrying pike and pistol. Leave those to men who are born to protect you and make you happy.*[70]

This is not to say that women did not play important roles in the Revolution, for they did. Groups of women often demonstrated in the streets or rioted over food shortages and the cost of bread. The dramatic march on Versailles on October 5, 1789—organized and led by the working-class women and other women of Paris—was a noteworthy example. However, in large degree, such activities were extensions of traditional women's social roles. Women had long been "purchasers of and negotiators for

Women's protests were rarely violent, though often threatening, seeking to jolt men into action. Ordinary women acted mostly as consumers, but they linked this with politics in sophisticated ways.

bread in the marketplace," British historian Olwen Hufton wrote. "Not only were they sensitive to prices, but they had a special role to play in defense of the consumer interests of the family ... Women believed themselves invested with specific (and never defined) powers to riot [to promote those interests] without incurring legal action if certain rules [such as not destroying anyone's property] were respected."[71]

At a slightly more wealthy socioeconomic level, the salon was another key institution in which women played a central role. Salons provided a place for women and men to congregate for intellectual conversation, including political dialogue. In a male-dominated society, women served as the host (*salonniere*), set the agenda of topics to be considered, and regulated the discussion. This led to reduced marginalization of women in Paris.

Only a handful of women and men lobbied for political rights for women. Among them was Condorcet, who in 1790, helped establish the Social Circle, a group that campaigned for female equality. The most daring advocate of women's rights during the Revolution was Marie Gouze, better known by her pen name, Olympe de Gouges. In September 1791, she published *The Declaration of the Rights of Woman and of the Citizen*, which stated in part:

> *Woman is born free and remains equal to man in rights ...*
>
> *The law should be the expression of the general will. All citizenesses and citizens should take part, in person or by their representatives, in its formation. It must be the same for everyone. All citizenesses and citizens, being*

Women formed clubs during the Revolution to discuss politics, especially in regard to safety, but these were shut down by the government.

equal in its eyes, should be equally admissible to all public dignities, offices and employments, according to their ability, and with no other distinction than that of their virtues and talents.[72]

Such efforts to advance women's political rights did not garner much support. French women did not obtain the right to vote until much later, in 1944. However, it was in the 1790s, during the Revolution, that women and men at least began to awaken to the realization that women deserved the same natural rights as men and may someday enjoy equality under the law.

Secularizing Marriage

One social realm that underwent change to the benefit of women was marriage. The revolutionary deputies strongly felt that marriage should be taken out of the clergy's hands. "By secularizing marriage," Lynn Hunt wrote, "the state gained control over the civil registers (births, deaths, marriages) and replaced the Church as the ultimate authority in questions of family life."[73] Thus, the new government decreed that marriages had to be performed by a local government official. (If the bride and groom desired it, a priest could witness the ceremony.)

A more sweeping change was the legalization of divorce, which previously had not been allowed. As for the grounds, either a man or a woman could now seek a divorce if the spouse was insane, committed a major crime, abused his or her partner, repeatedly engaged in immoral acts, abandoned his or her partner for two years or more, or engaged in counterrevolutionary activities. In addition, by mutual consent, a husband and wife could claim they were incompatible and divorce after a six-month waiting period. Finally, all divorced persons were required to wait a year before remarrying. At the time, this was by far the most liberal divorce law in the world, and one of many ways the Revolution had brought about radical changes in French society.

Chapter Seven

THE END OF THE REVOLUTION: THE RISE OF NAPOLÉON

The execution of Robespierre and more than 100 of his colleagues and supporters brought the Reign of Terror to a crashing halt. However, while the Revolution did not end with their deaths, most of the legislators in the National Convention agreed that it had grown far too radical and the time had come to reassess their situation, which resulted in what is known as the Thermidorian Reaction. The mood of the National Convention had changed.

The National Convention neutralized the Committee of Public Safety, emptied the prisons of inmates who were arrested under the Law of Suspects, purged the Jacobin clubs, put Paris under the direct control of the national government, and welcomed the Girondists back into the fold. Perhaps the most drastic, and the most consequential, step taken by the new conservatives was the repeal of price controls that had kept a lid on the cost of food and necessities, causing prices to skyrocket. At the same time, the city of Paris slashed the size of bread rations for the poor. While rice was more easily available, the poor had no fuel for fires to cook it.

The legislators then turned their attention to the government itself. Clearly, they concluded, the Constitution of 1793 had been inadequate to meet the country's needs. A new one was called for that emphasized stability in the wake of the recent turmoil. In introducing this Constitution of 1795, François Boissy d'Anglas declared that the previous document had been "drafted by schemers, dictated by tyranny, and accepted through terror" and continued:

THE POLITICAL STRUCTURE OF THE DIRECTORY

The French Constitution of 1795 spelled out the political structure of the Directory. It stated the following about the five directors making up the executive branch:

The Executive Power shall be delegated to a Directory of five members appointed by the Legislative Body …

The Council of Five-Hundred shall prepare, by secret ballot, a list of [fifty potential] members of the Directory to be appointed, and shall present it to the Council of Elders, which shall choose, also by secret ballot, from said list.

The members of the Directory must be at least forty years of age.

They may be chosen only from among citizens who have been ministers or members of the Legislative Body …

The Directory shall be renewed in part by the election of one new member annually.

During the first four years, the order of retirement of those first elected shall be determined by lot.

None of the retiring members may be reelected until after an interval of five years.

Ancestors and descendants in direct line, brothers, uncles and nephews, first cousins, and those related by marriage … may not be members of the Directory at one and the same time.[1]

1. Quoted in "Constitution of the Year III (1795)," Liberty, Equality, Fraternity: Exploring the French Revolution. chnm.gmu.edu/revolution/d/450/.

Civil equality … is all that a reasonable man can claim. Absolute equality is a chimera; for it to exist one would have to assume complete equality in intelligence, virtue, physical strength, education, and fortune in all men … We must be governed by the best; and the best are those who are the most educated and most interested in the maintenance of laws: now, with very few exceptions, you find such men among those who, owning a piece of property, are devoted to the country that contains it, to the laws that protect it, to the tranquility that maintains it, and who owe to this property and to the economic security it provides the education that has made them capable of discussing with wisdom and exactitude the advantages and inconveniences of the laws that determine the fate of their native land. The man without property, on the other hand, requires a constant exercise of virtue to interest himself in a social order that preserves nothing for him, and to resist actions and movements that hold out hope to him ... A country governed by non proprietors is in a state of nature.[74]

In abandoning general equality, social rights, and many other Enlightenment principles, the Thermidorians made France a sort of modified republic that can better be described as an oligarchy. From ancient Greek words meaning "rule of the few," an oligarchy is a government in which a relatively small number of individuals share authority, each providing a check on the powers of the others. However, though this approach was well-meaning, time would prove it ineffective. The new leaders did such a good job of limiting their powers that they were unable to counter the steady rise of power in another quarter—the army. It would be a strong and irresistible military general who would eventually galvanize and stabilize the nation, finally bringing the Revolution to an end.

The Directory

The government ushered in by the new constitution acquired the general name the Directory, after one of its branches. It was intended to be a parliamentary system in which power would be shared between a legislative branch and an executive branch. To help avoid the kind of abuses that had occurred under the National Convention, the legislature was divided into two houses, each of which could check the powers of the other. One house, the Council of Five Hundred (with 500 members, as the name suggests), was given the authority to enact new laws. The other house, the Council of Ancients, had 250 members, each of whom had to be at least 40 years old. (However, in France between 1740 and 1790, the life expectancy of males was only between 24 and 28 years.) They could not make laws, but they could veto any laws made by the other house.

The executive branch, the Directory, consisted of five men of equal status and authority. They were chosen by the Ancients from among the ranks of the 500. To help keep a single executive from amassing too much power, one of the five men was required to retire each year, so that the longest any one director could serve was five years.

The Constitution of 1795 also put new limits on the people's voting rights in an attempt to make voters more responsible and discourage mob mentality and violence. For example, only male citizens with a certain amount of property, along with all soldiers, were permitted to vote for members of the two legislative houses. Women and the poor were still excluded from voting. Also, as the following constitutional provisions indicate, certain restraints were placed on the rights to assemble and redress grievances:

> *No private society [group] which concerns itself with political questions may correspond with another, or affiliate therewith, or hold public sessions composed of the members of the societies and of associates distinguished from one another, or impose conditions of admission and eligibility, or arrogate [claim] to itself rights of exclusion, or cause its members to wear any external insignia of their association … Citizens may exercise their political rights only in the primary or communal assemblies …*
>
> *All citizens shall be free to address petitions to the public authorities, but they must be individual ones; no association may present them collectively, except the constituted authorities, and only for matters within their competence.*
>
> *The petitioners must never forget the respect due the constituted authorities.*[75]

The Overreach of the Military

The Directory appeared to be more or less adequate to the task of governing France, at least for the moment. However, the legislators and directors were totally inadequate to the job of fighting the foreign war that still raged outside the country's borders. Fortunately for the French, the tide in that conflict had turned, mostly in France's favor, in the recent past. French armies had overrun Belgium and annexed its territories to northern France, the Dutch had surrendered, and both Prussia and Spain had made peace with the French. Thus, in the closing weeks of 1795, Austria and Britain were the last major European powers still at war with France.

Still, the Austrians and British were extremely formidable foes who could potentially defeat the French on their own. The Directory had to take the ongoing war seriously and try to achieve either victory or a negotiated peace favorable to France. To accomplish such goals, the national leaders in Paris had no choice but to rely on the power of the army, including both the generals and soldiers under their command. However, this reliance came at a high price, as the military became increasingly powerful and the government, in turn, became more and more dependent on its good will. As scholar Donald Kagan wrote, "The growing role of the [French revolutionary] army held profound consequences not only for France but for the entire world."[76]

The newfound power of the French troops derived partly from the fact that each and every one of them could vote (while French citizens that were women or too poor to own property could not). Collectively speaking, therefore, the soldiers made up a powerful part of the national electorate. Also, and more ominously, most of the troops were no longer animated by the fiery revolutionary zeal they had exhibited in the Revolution's first couple of years. Increasingly, they felt more allegiance to their generals in the field than to the Revolution's leaders in the distant city of Paris. "The tradition of antagonism toward king, priests, and nobles, was still strong" among the soldiers, Christopher Hibbert wrote. However, "spirits in the ranks were no longer kept up by enthusiasm for the republican cause. [The troops] felt pride in their regiments and in French might rather than in the Revolution. It was their generals they looked to for leadership now, not the civilians at home."[77]

As for these generals, many were young, ambitious, and eager both to prove themselves in battle and to become powerful national figures. According to Australian scholar Martyn Lyons:

> *The republican army offered rapid promotion to talented and ambitious individuals. Deaths, emigration, and dismissals opened up new avenues for social advancement. Many soldiers … rose to high positions at a comparatively young age … [Louis-Lazare] Hoche, for example, son of a [mule keeper], was a general at the age of twenty-six, and [Pierre-François] Augereau, son of a [fruit vendor], emerged from humble origins to become a general in his thirties.*[78]

Although the leaders of the Directory worried about the growing power of the generals, they felt that, in the long run, they would be able to contain that power in the name of the Revolution. However, this proved to be a grave error.

The Italian Campaign

The first major sign of the Directory's underestimation of the threat the military posed came during the military campaigns of 1796 to 1797. French leaders felt that the most logical and efficient way to defeat the Austrians was to attack them on two major fronts. The first would consist of a thrust at Austria's capital, Vienna, from Germany. The other assault would come from the south, mainly Italy. At the time, Italy was not the united nation it is today. Instead, it was a patchwork of small states—some independent, others controlled by various European powers, including Austria. One of the French generals, Napoléon Bonaparte, presented the Directory with a plan for swiftly conquering a large portion of Italy. It would, he argued, put France in an excellent position to go forward with its attack on Austria.

Napoléon, as he is most often called today, was a brilliant, ambitious individual who had been born on the Mediterranean island of Corsica, a French territory. As a young man, he had trained as an artillery officer. Later, with the Revolution in full swing, he had supported the Jacobins and become a close associate of Robespierre. In October 1795, Napoléon commanded a force of government troops who put down a group of counterrevolutionaries in Paris, an episode that made him a famous hero of the Revolution.

With the consent of the Directory, in March 1796, Napoléon—now a general—took charge of about 38,000 French troops and headed for Italy. On March 27, he told his men:

> *Soldiers, you are naked, ill fed! The Government owes you much; it can give you nothing. Your patience, the courage you display in the midst of these rocks, are admirable; but they procure you no glory, [and] no fame is reflected upon you. I seek to lead you into the most fertile plains in the world. Rich provinces, great cities will be in your power. There you will find honor, glory, and riches.*[79]

This idealistic depiction of French troops entering Rome in 1798 highlights the heroism of the soldiers.

COUP D'ÉTAT: NOVEMBER 1799

Several years after his eventual fall from power, Napoléon recalled in his memoirs some of the events of the coup that had brought him that power on November 9, 1799.

> *[I] entered the Council of Ancients and placed [myself] at the bar, opposite to the president. "You stand," [I] said, "upon a volcano. The Republic no longer possesses a government. The Directory is dissolved. Factions are at work. The hour of decision has come. You have called in my arm, and the arms of my comrades to the support of your wisdom ... I desire nothing but the safety of the Republic!" ... The force of this speech, and [my] energy, brought over three-quarters of the members of the Council, who rose to indicate their [approval] ... then [I then went to the Council of Five Hundred, where at first the deputies] rose, crying, "Death to the Dictator!" ... The drum put an end to the clamor. [My] soldiers entered the chamber [with their] bayonets [raised]. The deputies leaped out the windows and dispersed, leaving their gowns, caps, etc. In one moment, the chamber was empty.*[1]

The coup d'état of 18 Brumaire (November 9, 1799) brought General Napoléon Bonaparte to power as First Consul of France, and ended the Revolution.

1. Quoted in Napoléon Bonaparte, *Memoirs of the History of France During the Reign of Napoléon, Dictated by the Emperor, Vol. 1.* London, UK: Henry Colburn, 1823, pp. 93-98.

The troops soon found Napoléon to be a man of his word as well as a gifted military strategist. He led them to a series of stunning victories that secured large sections of Italy for France. Also, and crucially, he boldly took the initiative and conducted what amounted to his own personal foreign policy, negotiating with the enemy without consulting his bosses in the Directory. For example, he concluded a treaty with Austria in the autumn of 1797, which resulted in that nation making peace and dropping out of the war. Soon afterward, he brought all of Italy and Switzerland under French domination.

These events had significant consequences both for Napoléon himself and for the leaders of the French government. "The Italian campaign," according to Lyons, "did not only make Bonaparte an illustrious commander, it also transformed him into a figure of political importance in European affairs."[80] The members of the Directory, still a weak and indecisive body, now found themselves in an unexpected and very awkward position. Although they did not like having a general who exercised so much independent authority, they could not afford to openly oppose a winning commander of such high stature. The Directory "could not argue with a general who delivered such spectacular victories and war booty," Lyons pointed out, so "they reluctantly accepted his decisions." Napoléon was now "a continental military statesman as well as a military commander and, for him, this constituted a double victory—that of the French over the Austrians, and that of Bonaparte over the civilian government."[81]

Tumultuous Series of Transformations

In the two years that followed, Napoléon proceeded to increase his power and

The Battle of the Pyramids in Egypt on July 21, 1798, was a crucial victory for Napoléon.

reputation even further. He wanted to strike at the British as hard as possible and decided that the most effective way would be to invade Egypt. The goods from Britain's most lucrative colony, India, moved into Europe by passing through Egypt, which was then a province of the Ottoman Turkish Empire. Napoléon went ahead with the Egyptian expedition early in 1798. He soon lost most of his fleet to British warships. Nevertheless, his army was successful on land, and he began exploiting the country, once again acting mainly on his own initiative.

Most other Europeans were alarmed at the French invasion of Egypt. In response, in December 1798, Britain, Austria, Russia, Portugal, and Turkey formed a new anti-French alliance, the so-called Second Coalition. Not long before, a priest-led uprising had broken out in French-ruled Belgium. In Paris, the already fragile and widely unpopular Directory was now confronted with more problems than it could handle.

The opportunistic Napoléon wasted no time in taking advantage of the Directory's weakness. He agreed to play a major role in a military coup against the government. Engineering the plot with him were the former revolutionary Abbé Sieyès, who by that time had risen to become one of the Directory's five members, another director, Charles Maurice de Talleyrand, and Napoléon's bother, Lucien, leader of the Council of Five Hundred.

The new government came to be known as the Consulate, based on the title Consul, which was the name of the administrator-generals of the ancient Roman Republic. Legislation would be created by three citizen assemblies. At first, Sieyès thought he would be the controlling member of the Consulate. However, Napoléon assumed that coveted role by drafting a new constitution and, over the course of several months, manipulating both people and laws to attain the position of "First Consul"—essentially dictator of France.

Charles-Maurice de Talleyrand was a member of the small group that planned with Napoleon to overthrow the government.

ABRIDGING THE FREEDOM OF THE PRESS

After taking power in France, Napoléon counteracted the spirit of the freedom of the press the revolutionaries had fought for and introduced press censorship to help him maintain control of and reshape public opinion. In July 1801, he wrote to one of his secretaries, saying,

> *Citizen Ripault [Napoléon's librarian] is to see that he is supplied every day with all the papers that come out … He will read them carefully, make an abstract [summary] of everything they contain likely to influence public opinion, especially with regard to religion, philosophy, and political opinion. He will send me this abstract daily between five and six o'clock [a.m.].*
>
> *Once every ten days he will send me an analysis of all the books or pamphlets which have appeared during that period, calling attention to any passages on moral questions.*[1]

1. Quoted in Leon Bernard and Theodore B. Hodges, eds., *Readings in European History*. New York, NY: Macmillan, 1958, p. 350.

This chain of events ended the French Revolution. In the course of a decade, France had undergone a tumultuous series of transformations. It had evolved from monarchy to constitutional monarchy, then to constitutional republic, to near-anarchy, to oligarchy, and finally to military dictatorship. Napoléon himself delivered the Revolution's obituary, stating on December 15, 1799:

> *Frenchmen! A constitution is presented to you. It terminates the uncertainties which the provisional government had [recently] introduced … The Constitution is founded on the true principles of representative government, on the sacred rights of property, equality, and liberty … Citizens, the Revolution is established upon the principles which began it. It is ended.*[82]

Napoléon presented the war-weary French people with what appeared to be security and order. For the moment, most of them were willing to accept the offer. None among them foresaw that in the next several years, he would lead them to the very brink of European supremacy, and then, regrettably, into disaster's dark depths.

EPILOGUE

COMING TO TERMS WITH THE FRENCH REVOLUTION

When Napoléon declared in 1799 that the French Revolution was over, he was only partly right. True, the revolutionary speechmakers and activists—and their radical assemblies and political experiments—were gone. The revolutionaries' effort to establish representative democracy and equality was flawed, yet even after the end was declared, the spirit and fundamental principles of the Revolution were far from dead. Indeed, the Revolution changed the Western world forever. Historian R. R. Palmer wrote that the Revolution "became lodged in the collective memory, a past event with which each succeeding generation had to come to terms. Some lived in fear, and others in hope, that the giant was only sleeping and might be aroused."[83]

The Rise and Fall of Napoléon

The giant remained in relative slumber during the Napoléonic era, to be sure. After serving as First Consul for a few years, during which he dominated France's government, in 1804, Napoléon took the bold step of making himself emperor. He also pursued an extremely aggressive foreign policy. For several years, his armies defeated those of other European nations, creating a vast French empire. However, in 1815, an alliance of British, Austrian, and Prussian forces beat Napoléon at Waterloo in Belgium, and he was exiled to an island in the south Atlantic.

After Napoléon's fall, the defeated French restored the monarchy. However, they remembered the ideals of representative government that had emerged in the Revolution, so they placed certain constitutional limitations on royal power. Similarly, when King Louis-Philippe assumed the throne in 1830, he was forced to rule as a constitutional, rather than absolute, monarch. Even moderate monarchy proved unacceptable for many French, however. In 1848, they rose in a second revolution, dethroned King Louis-Philippe, and established their Second Republic.

During this new upheaval, France's sleeping giant woke. The original Declaration of Rights created by the revolutionaries of 1789 had not been forgotten, and it became a guiding force in shaping new laws and governmental institutions. A new constitution, framed in 1848, provided for a democratic republic with a president, elected legislature, separation of powers, and universal voting rights.

The World Had Been Watching

However, it was not only France that had been indoctrinated with these democratic ideals. The rest of the world had been watching, and during the first few decades of the 19th century, these ideals spread outward and took hold in various parts of Europe and beyond.

A new spirit of resistance to oppression slowly but steadily grew into a sort of powder keg of revolutionary zeal. The 1848 uprising in France supplied the spark to ignite that keg. In that same year, a series of revolutionary uprisings exploded across the continent in the widest geographic area of any revolution in modern Europe. As the Austrians forced their king from his throne, the Hungarians demanded and won a new constitution that recognized human rights. Nationalist activists also wanted to redraw the map of Europe, especially to unify Germany and Italy, each of which was made up of small city-states, states, and kingdoms.

The French Revolution generated powerful symbols—the language of politics, liberty, rights, and constitutions—that were eagerly appropriated, refashioned, and combined with local traditions and innovations across the map. It also encouraged thinking about nationalism in a new political universe, which challenged old monarchies worldwide. At this point, none of these nations completely abolished their old systems and set up open democracies. However, the seeds were planted that would later grow into the democratic Europe that emerged in the 20th century. As Carl Schurz, a German revolutionary (and later U.S. senator and Secretary of the Interior), wrote in his memoir:

> *Most of us indeed recoiled from the wild excesses which had stained with streams of innocent blood the national uprising in France during the Reign of Terror. But we hoped to stir up the national energies without such terrorism. At any rate the history of the French Revolution furnished to us models in plenty that mightily excited our imagination.*[84]

That struggle for a new system of civilization was also taking place in the Western Hemisphere. Citizens in Latin America drew inspiration from Enlightenment principles and news about the revolutions in France and the United States, even though Spain had tried to suppress those rebellious influences. Additionally, the French Revolution inspired Mexico's constitutions.

In this way, scholar Anthony Arblaster wrote, France's grand political and social experiments in the 1790s

> *transformed the modern history of democracy, [as] political ideas which had only been aspirations or dreams in the minds of [philosophers] or popular radicals, were placed on the agenda of real politics, not only in France or even Europe, but globally. The principles and example of the Revolution helped to inspire the first successful slave revolt in the Caribbean in Haiti, as well as the political independence movements of South America. All such movements raised the issue of democracy, of popular power.*[85]

Thus, by demonstrating that a country's people could dismantle its oppressive ancient order and rule themselves, the French Revolution helped to transform human civilization. It introduced new schools of thought into the political vocabulary—liberalism, conservatism, republicanism—and by leaving behind a newfound but lasting awareness that politics should never be concentrated solely in the hands of a few people, it provoked the endless desire for political power-sharing in 19th-century Europe and beyond. The triumph of democracy in the modern world (According to *The Economist* magazine, 116 nations have some form of democracy in 2015.) owes an incalculable debt to the French. The waves they "set in motion in 1789," Palmer remarked, "have sometimes been stormy, sometimes more tranquil, but never quite calm—nor does it seem likely that they will ever wholly subside."[86]

Notes

Introduction: "Man May Be Free, if He Resolves to Be So"

1. William Doyle, *The Oxford History of the French Revolution*. Oxford, UK: Clarendon, 2002, pp. 424–425.
2. Jacques Solé, *Questions of the French Revolution: A Historical Overview*, trans. Shelley Temchin. New York, NY: Pantheon, 1990, p. 236.
3. Doyle, *The Oxford History of the French Revolution*, p. 423.

Chapter One: Revolutionary Origins

4. Bronislaw Baczko, *"Enlightenment," A Critical Dictionary of the French Revolution*, Furet and Ozouf, eds. Cambridge, MA: Harvard University Press, 1989, p. 662.
5. William Doyle, *The French Revolution: A Very Short Introduction*. New York, NY: Oxford University Press, 2001, p. 19.
6. Arthur J. May, *A History of Civilization: The Mid-Seventeenth Century to Modern Times*. New York, NY: Scribners, 1964, p. 198.
7. Quoted in William Doyle, *Origins of the French Revolution*. Oxford, UK: Oxford University Press, 1999, p. 51.
8. Doyle, *The French Revolution: A Very Short Introduction*, p. 21.
9. May, *A History of Civilization*, pp. 192, 196.
10. Quoted in Doyle, *The Oxford History of the French Revolution*, p. 38.
11. May, *A History of Civilization*, p. 197.
12. George Rudé, *The French Revolution: Its Causes, Its History, and Its Legacy After 200 Years*. New York, NY: Weidenfeld and Nicolson, 1994, pp. 1–2.
13. John H. Stewart, ed., *A Documentary Survey of the French Revolution*. New York, NY: Macmillan, 1971, pp. 12–13.
14. Stewart, *A Documentary Survey of the French Revolution*, pp. 12–13.
15. Stewart, *A Documentary Survey of the French Revolution*, pp. 12–13.

Chapter Two: Political Awakening of 1789

16. Quoted in Laura Mason and Tracey Rizzo, *The French Revolution: A Document Collection*. Boston, MA: Houghton Mifflin, 1999, p. 50.

17. R.K. Gooch, *Parliamentary Government in France: Revolutionary Origins*, 1789–1791. New York, NY: Russell and Russell, 1971, p. 15.
18. Quoted in "Arthur Young's Travels in France During the Years 1787, 1788, 1789," Liberty Fund, Inc. oll.libertyfund.org/titles/young-arthur-youngs-travels-in-france-during-the-years-1787-1788-1789.
19. Christopher Hibbert, *The Days of the French Revolution*. New York, NY: Harper Collins, 1999, p. 49.
20. Quoted in Donald I. Wright, ed., *The French Revolution: Introductory Documents*. St. Lucia, QLD, Australia: University of Queensland Press, 1994, pp. 31–32.
21. Quoted in Mason and Rizzo, *The French Revolution*, p. 58.
22. Quoted in Wright, *The French Revolution*, pp. 2–3.
23. Quoted in Hibbert, *The Days of the French Revolution*, pp. 53–54.
24. Leo Gershoy, *The French Revolution and Napoléon*. New York, NY: Appleton-Century-Crofts, 1964, p. 109.
25. Quoted in Mason and Rizzo, *The French Revolution*, p. 59.
26. Quoted in Mason and Rizzo, *The French Revolution*, p. 61.

Chapter Three: Bloody Revolution

27. Quoted in Keith Michael Baker, *The Old Regime and the French Revolution*, Chicago, IL: The University of Chicago Press, 1987, p. 202.
28. Quoted in Mason and Rizzo, *The French Revolution*, p. 64.
29. Quoted in Mason and Rizzo, *The French Revolution*, p. 65.
30. Quoted in Hibbert, *The Days of the French Revolution*, p. 62.
31. Quoted in Hibbert, *The Days of the French Revolution*, pp. 63–64.
32. Quoted in Georges Pernoud and Sabine Flaissier, eds., *The French Revolution*, trans. Richard Graves. New York, NY: Capricorn, 1970, pp. 29–31.
33. Quoted in "A Defender of the Bastille Explains His Role," Liberty, Equality, Fraternity: Exploring the French Revolution. chnm.gmu.edu/ revolution/d/383/.
34. Doyle, *The Oxford History of the French Revolution*, pp. 110–111.
35. Doyle, *The Oxford History of the French Revolution*, p. 115.
36. Quoted in Hibbert, *The Days of the French Revolution*, p. 94.
37. Quoted in Stewart, *A Documentary Survey of the French Revolution*, p. 107.

Chapter Four: Spontaneous and Calculated Bloodshed

38. Quoted in Lynn Hunt, ed., *The French Revolution and Human Rights: A Brief Documentary History*. Boston, MA: St. Martin's, 1996, p. 15.
39. Quoted in Frank Maloy Anderson, ed., *The Constitutions and Other Select Documents Illustrative of*

the History of France, 1789–1907. New York, NY: Russell and Russell, 1967, pp. 59–60.

40. Quoted in Mason and Rizzo, *The French Revolution*, p. 104.
41. Hunt, *The French Revolution and Human Rights*, p. 15.
42. Quoted in Earl Leroy Higgins, ed., *The French Revolution as Told by Contemporaries*. Boston, MA: Houghton Mifflin, 1980, p. 130.
43. Quoted in Hunt, *The French Revolution and Human Rights*, pp. 93–94.
44. Mason and Rizzo, *The French Revolution*, p. 93.
45. David Andress, *The Terror: The Merciless War for Freedom in Revolutionary France*. New York, NY: Farrar, Straus and Giroux, 2005, p. 96.
46. Norah Lofts and Margery Weiner, *Eternal France: A History of France from the French Revolution Through World War II*. London, UK: Curtis Brown, 1968, p. 19.
47. Lofts and Weiner, Eternal France, pp. 19–20.

Chapter Five: Revolution in Crisis

48. Peter McPhee, *Living the French Revolution, 1789–1799*. London, UK: Palgrave Macmillan, 2009, p. 132.
49. R. R. Palmer, *Twelve Who Ruled: The Year of the Terror in the French Revolution*. Princeton, NJ: Princeton University Press, 1941, 1989, p. 5.
50. Richard T. Bienvenu, ed., *The Ninth of Thermidor: The Fall of Robespierre*. Oxford, UK: Oxford University Press, 1970, p. 49.
51. Quoted in Stewart, *A Documentary Survey of the French Revolution*, p. 472.
52. R. F. Leslie, *The Age of Transformation, 1789 to 1871*. New York, NY: Harper and Row, 1967, p. 50.
53. Quoted in Higgins, *The French Revolution as Told by Contemporaries*, p. 307.
54. Quoted in Wright, *The French Revolution*, pp. 154–155.
55. Quoted in Stewart, *A Documentary Survey of the French Revolution*, p. 478.
56. Quoted in Anderson, *The Constitutions and Other Selected Documents*, pp. 154–156.
57. Hibbert, *The Days of the French Revolution*, pp. 226–227.
58. Quoted in Hibbert, *The Days of the French Revolution*, p. 222.
59. Quoted in Henry Morse Stephens, *The Principal Speeches of the Statesmen and Orators of the French Revolution, 1789–1795*, vol. 2. Oxford, UK: Clarendon, 1892, p. 275.
60. Quoted in John Paxton, *Companion to the French Revolution*. New York, NY: Facts on File, 1989, p. 166.
61. Quoted in Higgins, *The French Revolution as Told by Contemporaries*, p. 357.

Chapter Six: Revolutionary Culture and Society

62. Lynn Hunt, *Politics, Culture, and Class in the French Revolution.* Berkeley, CA: University of California Press, 1984, p. 29.
63. Emmet Kennedy, *A Cultural History of the French Revolution.* New Haven, CT: Yale University Press, 1991, p. 145.
64. Quoted in Mason and Rizzo, *The French Revolution,* p. 104.
65. Quoted in Kennedy, *A Cultural History of the French Revolution*, p. 150.
66. Hibbert, *The Days of the French Revolution*, pp. 231–233.
67. Quoted in "Religion: The Cult of the Supreme Being," Liberty, Equality, Fraternity: Exploring the French Revolution. chnm.gmu.edu/revolution/d/436/.
68. Quoted in Stewart, *A Documentary Survey of the French Revolution*, pp. 369–370.
69. Quoted in "Primary Schools," Liberty, Equality, Fraternity: Exploring the French Revolution. chnm.gmu.edu/revolution/d/464/.
70. Quoted in Doyle, *The Oxford History of the French Revolution*, pp. 420–421.
71. Olwen Hufton, "Voilà la Citoyenne," *History Today*, May 1989, pp. 27–28.
72. Quoted in Olympe de Gouges, "The Declaration of the Rights of Woman," Liberty, Equality, Fraternity: Exploring the French Revolution. chnm.gmu.edu/revolution/d/293/.
73. Lynn Hunt, "The Unstable Boundaries of the French Revolution," in Philippe Ariès and Georges Duby, eds., *A History of Private Life, vol. 4: From the Fires of Revolution to the Great War*, trans. by Arthur Goldhammer. ed. Michelle Perrot. Cambridge, MA: Harvard University Press, 1990, p. 30.

Chapter Seven: The End of the Revolution: The Rise of Napoléon

74. Doyle, *The Oxford History of the French Revolution*, p. 318.
75. Quoted in "Constitution of the Year III (1795)," Liberty, Equality, Fraternity: Exploring the French Revolution. chnm.gmu.edu/revolution/d/430/.
76. Donald Kagan, Steven Ozment, and Frank M. Turner, *The Western Heritage.* New York, NY: Prentice-Hall, 2006, p. 672.
77. Hibbert, *The Days of the French Revolution*, p. 295.
78. Martyn Lyons, *Napoléon Bonaparte and the Legacy of the French Revolution.* New York, NY: St. Martin's Press, 1994, p. 16.
79. Quoted in "Napoléon's Proclamation to His Troops in Italy (March–April 1796)," The History Guide. www.historyguide.org/intellect/nap1796.html.
80. Lyons, *Napoléon Bonaparte,* p. 15.

81. Lyons, *Napoléon Bonaparte,* pp. 24–25.
82. Quoted in Stewart, *A Documentary Survey of the French Revolution*, p. 780.

Epilogue: Coming to Terms with the French Revolution

83. Robert R. Palmer, *The World of the French Revolution*. New York, NY: HarperCollins, 1972, p. 251.
84. Carl Schurz, "Reminiscences of a Long Life," *McClure's Magazine vol. 26*, 1906, p. 372.
85. Anthony Arblaster, *Democracy*. Philadelphia, PA: Open University Press, 2002, p. 38.
86. Palmer, *The World of the French Revolution*, p. 270.

For More Information

Books

Andress, David. *The Terror: The Merciless War for Freedom in Revolutionary France.* New York, NY: Farrar, Straus and Giroux, 2005.

This is a dramatic new interpretation of the French Revolution that draws troubling parallels with today's political and religious fundamentalism.

Doyle, William. *The Oxford History of the French Revolution.* Oxford, UK: Clarendon, 2002.

Doyle is a great scholar of the Revolution, and this is one of the most comprehensive and reliable existing overviews of the Revolution.

Mason, Laura, and Tracey Rizzo. *The French Revolution: A Document Collection.* Boston, MA: Houghton Mifflin, 1999.

A useful collection of primary sources about the Revolution, this book gives readers a taste of what it was really like in France during the chaotic late–18th century.

Moore, Lucy. *Liberty: The Lives and Times of Six Women in Revolutionary France.* New York, NY: HarperCollins, 2007.

Lucy Moore paints a vivid portrait of six Frenchwomen from vastly different social and economic backgrounds who helped stoke the fervor and idealism of the Revolution, and who risked everything to make their mark on history.

Schama, Simon. *Citizens: A Chronicle of the French Revolution.* New York, NY: Knopf, 2005.

This book gives a large, sprawling treatment of the subject with a controversial slant—that the Revolution was driven more by the self-delusion and violent acts of a few leaders than by the French people and their desire for liberty.

Scurr, Ruth. *Fatal Purity: Robespierre and the French Revolution.* London, UK: Chatto & Windus, 2006.

A timely reminder of just how perilous and fragile the journey from tyranny to political freedom has been—and indeed still is—in so many countries today, this book helps draw parallels between history and modern times.

Tackett, Timothy, *The Coming of the Terror in the French Revolution.* Cambridge, MA: Belknap Press, 2015.

Exploring the mentality of the revolutionaries on the eve of the Reign of Terror,

Tackett reveals how suspicion and mistrust escalated and helped propel their actions, ultimately consuming them and the Revolution itself.

Websites

French Revolution

www.history.com/topics/french-revolution

The interactive History Channel website has links to clips from their series on the Revolution and accompanying short articles. It also has multimedia learning tools, such as historical reenactments, to help bring the Revolution to life.

Liberty, Equality, Fraternity: Exploring the French Revolution

chnm.gmu.edu/revolution

This collaboration of scholars from George Mason University and the City University of New York is possibly the best general site about the Revolution on the Internet. In addition to historical overviews, it contains hundreds of primary source documents pertaining to the Revolution.

Marie Antoinette and the French Revolution

www.pbs.org/marieantoinette/index.html

Despite being such a controversial figure during the Revolution, Marie-Antoinette remains one of its most fascinating figures, and this site provides a timeline of her life, extending beyond just her trial and execution.

Napoleon

www.pbs.org/empires/napoleon/home.html

Produced by PBS, this site has brief, but useful, overviews on a variety of topics related to Napoléon, ranging from the background of the man himself to the politics of his wife.

"5 Myths About the French Revolution"

www.washingtonpost.com/opinions/5-myths-about-the-french-revolution/2015/07/09/6f27c6f0-25af-11e5-b72c-2b7d516e1e0e_story.html

This brief article is a fun and interesting look at how the French Revolution has come to be understood and misunderstood in modern times.

Index

H

I

J

K

L

M

N

O

P

R

S

T

V

W

Y

Picture Credits

Cover, pp. 15, 18, 24, 37, 50, 64 Heritage Images/Contributor/Hulton Fine Art Collection/Getty Images; pp. 6-7 (background), 6 (middle) Everett Historical/ Shutterstock.com; pp. 6 (left and right), 22 Courtesy of the Library of Congress; pp. 7 (left), 25 Bettmann/Contributor/Bettmann/Getty Images; pp. 7 (right), 10, 41, 52, 85 UniversalImagesGroup/Contributor/Universal Images Group/Getty Images; p. 9 Georgios Kollidas/Shutterstock.com; p. 11 Niday Picture Library/ Alamy Stock Photo; pp. 13, 48 HultonArchive/Stringer/Hulton Archive/Getty Images; p. 14, Print Collector/Contributor/Hulton Fine Art Collection/Getty Images; pp. 17, 53, 76 adoc-photos/Contributor/Corbis Historical/Getty Images; p. 19 Lepicie, Nicolas-Bernard (1735-84)/Musee des Beaux-Arts, Rennes, France/ Bridgeman Images; pp. 20, 72 Culture Club/Contributor/Hulton Archive/Getty Images; p. 27 Frederic Legrand - COMEO/Shutterstock.com; p. 28 De Agostini Picture Library/Contributor/De Agostini/Getty Images; pp. 32, 59 Leemage/ Contributor/Corbis Historical/Getty Images; p. 35 DEA / G. DAGLI ORTI/ Contributor/De Agostini/Getty Images; p. 39 Hulton Archive/Handout/Hulton Archive/Getty Images; pp. 42, 60 Heritage Images/Contributor/Hulton Archive/ Getty Images; pp. 45, 54 PHAS/Contributor/Universal Images Group/Getty Images; pp. 47, 51, 63, 83 Photo 12/Contributor/Universal Images Group/Getty Images; pp. 55, 84 Print Collector/Contributor/Hulton Archive/Getty Images; p. 57 Adwo/Shutterstock.com; pp. 58, 65 ullstein bild/Contributor/ullstein bild/ Getty Images; p. 69 Universal History Archive/Contributor/Universal Images Group/Getty Images; p. 75 French School, (18th century)/Musee de la Ville de Paris, Musee Carnavalet, Paris, France/Archives Charmet/Bridgeman Images; p. 86 Buyenlarge/Contributor/Hulton Fine Art Collection/Getty Images.

About the Author

A former university administrator and strong proponent of lifelong learning, **Karen Haywood** has copyedited books from many fiction and nonfiction genres including memoir, mystery, urban fantasy, alternate history, science fiction, and Westerns. She has written several books on endangered animals, U.S. state history, and human anatomy and physiology for young readers. An alumna of The University of North Carolina at Chapel Hill and Duke University, Ms. Haywood is proud to call North Carolina home.